Responding

Additional books by author:

Firehouse Fraternity Oral History Series:
Volume I: Becoming a Firefighter
Volume II: Life Between Alarms
Volume III: Equipment
Volume V: Riots to Renaissance
Volume VI: Changing the NFD

The Newark Riots: A View from the Firehouse

An Eerie Silence: An Oral History of Newark
Firefighters at the WTC

Hervey's Boys: New Jersey's First Chinese Community
1870-1886 (And What Happened After That)

Fiction:
The Firebox Stalker
The Hand Life Dealt you
A-zou: A Woman Living in Interesting Times

Children's Fiction:
A Hundred Battles (YA)
A Broken Glass (YA)
Balancing Act (Middle Grade)

The Firehouse Fraternity

An Oral History of the
Newark Fire Department

Volume IV

Responding

Neal Stoffers

Springfield and Hunterdon Publishing
Copyright 2009
www.newarkfireoralhistory.com

First Printing: 2009

ISBN: 978-1-970034-13-4

Springfield and Hunterdon Publishing
East Brunswick, NJ 08816-5852

Dedicated to past, present, and future generations of Newark firefighters, and especially to the 67 firefighters who made the ultimate sacrifice upholding their oath to protect the lives and property of Newark's citizens.

Contents

Acknowledgements

The credit for much of this book goes to the members of the Newark Fire Department who gave so generously of their time to take part in my oral history project. The hours of recorded conversations they contributed will help preserve the history of Newark's fire department and of Newark itself. A list of those interviewed appears at the end of the book. This is their story. I am honored to tell it.

Foreword

Responding is the fourth volume of the *Firehouse Fraternity, an Oral History of the Newark, New Jersey Fire Department.* In the first three volumes I have attempted to introduce the reader to Newark, her fire department, and the men who served her citizens from 1942 to 2003. If you have read any of the three previous books, you should have some idea of the type of men who manned Newark's firehouses; what they experienced in those firehouses; and the equipment they had available to do their job. This book is the first to move outside the controlled environment of the firehouse and into the streets of the city.

The titles of the last two chapters may need an explanation. Chapter four is entitled "The Price" because stories recounted in the previous volumes could give a reader the impression that what most of those I interviewed thought of as the best job in the world had only an up side. This chapter focuses on the down side of any fire department. These stories recount the sacrifices and suffering seen and experienced during the course of a fire service career. The final chapter "Four fours" derives its name from the telegraph signal sent over the bell system in firehouses when a brother firefighter dies. I leave it to the reader to judge whether the price paid by Newark's firefighters over the sixty-one years covered in this book was worth it.

As with the previous three volumes, this book recounts the experiences of Newark firefighters. These books tell the story of New Jersey's largest city and her fire department as seen through the eyes of the men manning her firehouses. I have attempted to group related subjects together to give the reader a true feel for various aspects of the fire service. The comments of the men I interviewed are presented in order of appointment date. This method is an attempt to give a better picture of the chronology of the dramatic changes which occurred in the city of Newark and the fire service in general.

The seeds of these books were unknowingly planted in a small firehouse on Springfield Avenue and Hunterdon Street. It was here as a young firefighter that I sat in the kitchen of Six Engine and listened to conversations between veteran firefighters, Captains, and Deputy Chiefs about a city and fire department that existed in another time.

In June of 1991, I began an oral history project to preserve the memories of these men and the generations of firefighters who followed. The purpose of this project was to capture not only the words, but the texture of their experiences. What was a firefighting career like during this period in Newark and by extrapolation in America? Fire departments across the country have shared the experiences of the NFD in one way or another. Whether read by a professional firefighter from New York City or by a volunteer firefighter from a small rural community, the stories will be familiar. The fire service is a small world with a common purpose.

I hope what is recorded here will show both a bygone era and the evolution of the Newark Fire Department into its present form. If others outside the fire service walk away with a better understanding of the firefighters and the fire departments that protect them, my time over the past years will have been well spent.

Chapter One: Tactics

Fredette: (appointed 1942) The engine would pull up to the hydrant. The wagon was behind the engine. A man would hop off the wagon with a two and a half and hook up to the engine. Then we would stretch with the hose wagon. We would stretch the booster in if it only called for a booster. If not, we would break the connection and put a hose into the pump outlet. You would take your two and half inch line in.

We also had a Heffernan valve. It was a big aluminum thing that you would hook up to the hydrant, stretch, and then later on you could hook up two and a half and bypass it. You had two two and a half outlets. Then you had the big suction. So, your engine would be hooked up to this Heffernan valve. But in the mean time you would be getting water from the two and a half inch outlet of the Heffernan valve. Then when the engine had time they would hook up to the big outlet of the Heffernan valve, switch over, and shut off the two and a half going into the pump. But it wasn't a good piece of equipment because there were only a few of them in the city. If you had a detail man in your company, he knew nothing about it. I remember one guy took his rubber coat off and threw it over the Heffernan valve because he had everything all screwed up. I think a fire chief in New York created it. It was a good piece of equipment if everybody was properly trained, but nobody bothered with it.

The main thing was you had to have that two and a half. We went into the building. We didn't fight fires from the outside. We went in. We went in with the booster and if you had a good truck company, they would give you protection by ventilating for you.

When I went to Six Engine, we stretched lines and the booster. You'd put your finger over the nozzle to get what we called the Captain Reiss spray. Captain Reiss was in Twelve Engine. He used to have the celluloid collar and a little tie on at all fires. He never wore a mask and could take smoke. We used to put out more portable oil heater fires with our finger on that nozzle with that spray than all these CO^2 extinguishers and all these fancy extinguishers you have.

Vetrini: (appointed 1946) If the engine took the hydrant the hose wagon had to stretch into the fire. If the engine went past the fire to go to the hydrant, they would drop off the hose. Because we had men on both rigs, one and four, one and five, with two platoons. Sometimes you would roll with two on the wagon and one on the engine, besides your driver and the Captain.

Redden: (appointed 1947) You pull up to working fire. If you had a hydrant beyond the fire, you would stretch with the rig because on one side you had the male hose coupling sticking out; on the other side you had the female. So, you could either stretch to the fire or away from the fire. If the hydrant is on the other end, you would stretch with the rig and you would have your play-pipe right at the fire. Just reverse it if you have to stop at the hydrant before the fire. Then you would stretch in by hand. On the second alarm, you try to stretch from a company that was hooked up.

Kinnear: (appointed 1947) Frankly, I don't think the tactics have changed. A guy grabs a line or two guys grab a line, bring it in the front door, up to the fire, and throw some water on it. The truck company goes to the roof and ventilates. The methods haven't really changed. Of course, there have been refinements in nozzles and refinements in tools. The equipment has changed and some of the theories of fighting fire, but the basic method is still the same.

Masters: (appointed 1947) The truck had an understanding with the engine. We worked together. The front of the fire building was left vacant. I could pull in and turn the apparatus. Whichever way the ladder was going, you turned the cab the opposite. The tillerman took the tiller seat off and swung it around. He would hop off, pull out the jack. Whichever way the aerial was going, that's the jack you pull out first. Then you did the other side. After that I'd raise my ladder to the roof or if there were people at the windows, the windows.

F. Grehl: (appointed 1948) You have to make a survey of the situation and then determine which of the factors have to be taken care of. Obviously, life hazard's always first. Then you go into what activities are needed to take care of the life hazard. Whether it would be a hose stream to protect them or get a ladder. If you were an engine company and you didn't have a ladder high enough as we did in the beginning, there was only one thing to do. Someone stands there and keeps talking to the people, "We're coming, we're coming." Get inside, control the inside stairways. Because many a time in Six Engine you didn't have the ladders to reach the people. The only way to get them was to get inside, control the stairways, get to the room where they were, and get them out that way. Make your size up when you get to the fire, life hazard first and then exposures, whether they're exterior exposures or interior exposures.

If you stretch a two and a half inch line, you need a few more men. You can stretch an inch and a half with two guys. But you stretch a two and a half, you need at least three, depending on how high you're going. You just can't have one guy in the stairwell, another guy on the nozzle and a little excess hose with a two and a half. You need people all over the place. One of the things we did with two and a half was go up the stairwell and try to feed it up that way, but it was very, very heavy when charged. Basically we were taught to lay it on the stairs because it took away from that excess weight. One of the training things we had later was to put a hose strap underneath a coupling and wrap it around a railing to take the weight off of it. When we got the inch and a half, the weight wasn't there, so we got away from that. You don't see hose straps used anywhere. It's very rare, but that was a mandatory thing years back.

There's no way we can change the basics because the most economical method we have of putting out fires is water. In order to give the water, we have the same basic principles. We try to improve the equipment to reduce the friction loss so you have better pressure, better volume, and things of that nature. Inch and three quarter hose today with the proper pressure, with rapid water gives you as much water as two and a half inch hose. That's a tremendous improvement and there was a budget savings. One reason why we often ride one and two is the fellows can do the job. That was the important thing. It didn't make any difference how many people you had. They always seemed to do the job. They gave that little extra. The job always managed to get done.

One thing that helped cut down on fires involving six, eight buildings, which came to an abrupt halt, was our change in fire tactics. It was another experimental thing which I think we learned from the volunteers and the riots, where we really did it, that was the quick use of master streams. We can pre-connect an inch and a half line. With five hundred gallons of water now, why can't we pre-connect the master stream? We started to do that and we were able to stop a lot of fires from extending.

McCormack: (appointed 1949) Standard operating procedures in those days were when you pulled up to a building, if you saw smoke or a small amount of fire like a bedroom fire or a couch fire you would stretch your booster into the building. The first due company would take the booster in. The expression in those days was the first due company ran free, meaning basically that they would gather information. If they stretched a booster in and there was really a serious fire in the building, they weren't penalized for it because they didn't know until they got there.

The second due company was mandated if they saw a booster going into the front door of the building when they pulled up, to stretch a two and a half inch line right up the front porch and back up the booster. You didn't necessarily have to wet it, but you had to have a two and a half inch line at the front porch. If they needed more water, an additional line, you would bring the two and a half in. If you didn't get that two and a half up there to back up that first due company, you were in serious trouble with the chief.

We had a one inch booster line with a straight tip when I first came on. No fog tip; there was no such thing. We had the straight tip, a straight pipe on the booster line. In order to get fog, we were taught to shot the line up at the ceiling. It would hit the ceiling, break up, and come down in a spray form. Or we were taught to put our thumb over the stream and break it up in that fashion, to convert it into droplets and make your own fog nozzle. The back up to that, as I mentioned earlier, was the two and a half inch line. There was no fog nozzle on that either, straight tip play pipe. That's all we had. That's what we worked with. If it was a large fire, a fire of any great volume, you worked with two and a half inch lines. If you rolled in and saw a factory or a large volume of fire even in a three story frame, everyone who came in would stretch two and a half inch lines, outside of the first due company. If you came in on a second alarm, the chief might tell you to take a booster into the building next door to cover the exposure or check. But the basic fires were fought with big lines, so obviously we were very destructive. I mean it was impossible not to be. Picture a five or six room apartment in a three-story frame house. Picture a two and a half in there. It's like Niagara Falls going through the hose. If the fire didn't destroy it we did, but it was all we had. We didn't know any better at the time.

Masterson: (appointed 1949) I rode on the back step of the wagon. We rode in and it was according to if we were first due. If we have a working job, the wagon would pull up alongside the hydrant. I'd throw a line on the hydrant and then get back on and take off with the wagon. We'd go down and we'd pull out the hose we needed. The captain would be right there with it and nine out of ten times, you knew we were going in the front door. That's where the fire was. We'd go in and the driver would hook up. If you had a guy on the back step of the engine, he'd be over there working with it. The driver would hook up the line in and out of the wagon.

Most of the time, you hooked up to the engine. You'd signal to the engine guys, charge it. Okay, I'm hooked up, open the line. Before even that, you'd shoot the water out to the guys inside. We'd work off the tank. The driver was just hoping that water gets here from the engine fast enough to back them up. Sometimes when you were working inside, working with a line, all of the sudden it would go down and it'll come back up. That's the connection coming through. You would hook up inch and a half to the wagon, and then the feed line would come in. You had to have a feed line with inch and a half or you'd empty that tank in no time at all.

If the wagon was out of service, we'd pull up in front of the fire building with the engine, drop off on the ground what we needed and the engine would take off from there. Instead of going from the hydrant to the fire, we'd go from the fire to the hydrant. So, you could get out of there when the fire was out without getting hung up. If you had stopped the engine in front of the building and you had no wagon, you had to drag the feed by hand and that's a lot of work. This way you could just pull up in front of the fire building and pull out whatever hose you needed. You've got a three story frame. You know just about how much inch and a half you need. You could hook it on to a two and a half with a reducer on it. Let the engine go. That's if you don't have the wagon. Sometimes if it's close enough, you'll go all inch and a half. If the hydrant's right there, of course, it's just inch and a half. But if you have a long stretch, you might as well run a two and a half down the street for the water. If it was a small fire, just a little smoke, we didn't stretch. We'd pull up there and I'd grab the booster and take off, whoever rode the back step of the wagon. You'd pull it up there. The captain was there. He'd be right along with you, helping you along and he'd see where you were at. He was in charge. That was your job, to do the work. He wouldn't take the line off you because that would only make you mad. He would help you with the line, but he wouldn't take it off you because guys didn't like to give up the line. That was the big thing in those days, not to give up the line. You'd fight over the line. You'd do all kinds of tricks with Twenty Engine, Six Engine. They were always battling heads to screw the other guy up. But that was it. The competition at the fire never got nasty. Every time you go to a fire, a racket, a retirement affair or a promotional affair, everybody was partying, everybody was friends. Just one guy trying to tell a bigger lie than the other, that's all.

Deutch: (appointed 1953) We had pretty good procedures at Five Truck. One man would grab the sixteen foot ladder and go around and ventilate the windows on the second floor, knock them out. Two men would go in. One man would go out to the back. If it was an aerial job, you'd raise it. Two men would go to the roof. All the rest would go inside after they ventilated the outside. We didn't have the masks though.

Wall: (appointed 1954) The first due truck took the front of the building, did the obvious, rescue, ventilation, or whatever. The second due truck took the rear. And you began your primary search in the rear of the building, start working your way down. The Captain took two guys with him. The tillerman and driver were responsible for the roof, working your way down from there. That was pretty much the way I've always seen it operate.

Freeman: (appointed 1956) We'd pull off the inch and a half and just go right in. We had pre-connected, and they'd give us the tank. I think we had three hundred gallons in the Mack.

McGee: (appointed 1956) None of the procedures have changed really because the situations don't change for fires overall. Your job is to put the fire out. The only thing that would be different is a lot of companies had what they called hose companies. They were two-piece companies. They had the engine, which they used as a pumper and a hose wagon, which basically carried hose, but did have pumps on them, too. In the event of a fire usually the hose wagon would precede the engine from the firehouse, drop their hose off at the hydrant, and stretch into the front of the fire building. The engine would hook up at the hydrant that they stretched from and pump. You had to have some manpower to do that. Most companies that were two-piece had seven or eight men assigned to them. That was the normal operating procedure. The first due company got in front of the building and tried to give a report of what was going on. The chiefs by that time would be on the scene. It would be the responsibility of the second, third, and fourth due companies to supply most of the water or at least be in position to supply the water.

Most of the time, you would stretch a booster. If somebody saw you stretching a booster in, they would stretch a two and a half inch line to back it up. Maybe not charge it, but you would stretch it. It was usually the same safe guards that are in place today. If you see people with a booster, they'll stretch an inch and a half. They switched to inch and a half prior to the riots. So it had to be in that time frame between 1957 and '67, somewhere in there, maybe in the early '60s. They went from the two and a half to the inch and a half.

By the time of the riots the typical Newark operation of the first due engine pulling up and working off the tank with the inch and half was in place. Because the combination of the bigger booster tank and inch and a half line gave us the ability to get almost three minutes of a stream. If it was used halfway sparingly, maybe even five minutes from an inch and a half line off a five hundred gallon tank, which, in most cases, put out ninety percent of the fire. That was fairly common practice. By that time two other companies would have stretched their hoses in.

The truck companies would bring a twenty-four foot ladder to where the fire was and ladder the building. In those days the first due truck would ladder the building anyway, no matter where the fire was. Just to point out to the incoming companies that this was where the fire building was. That's pretty much done away with now. They called them markers. A lot of times there would be two or three buildings very close to each other. If it was a good fire, you couldn't tell which house it was in. So you would mark the building with a ladder. It would also serve as a second way out. But one of the principal reasons was to mark the building.

Raising the aerial would be secondary. It was for guys who go to the roof. Usually, if the fire was bad enough or it looked like it was going to be hard to find where the fire was, then they really wanted you to throw a ladder up someplace just in case anybody was still in the building on the second floor. It was probably one of your first operations, but you had more men then. That's chief to remember in this. You had the manpower to do this.

McGrory: (appointed 1956) We were using pre-connected when I came on, which was a good thing. But you used to run out of water, bang, like that. We didn't have the nozzles. The nozzles were another big improvement, constant flow gallonage. When I first became a captain, I used to go down and train with my guys. "How long you think we have on the tank?" We had it all figured out with different sprays and straight stream. We went down and timed everything so we knew what we had, which was very important to us.

Pre-connected inch and half lines with masks were a big advancement in firefighting. Newark used that quite a bit because we got in and you hit it. You might have a couple of rooms, but if you can get to it and do it, you're not going to have the surround and drown. I think that was what everybody in Newark tried to do. You didn't have to say it. You just knew it and you had to do it.

We started to use the Smith valve* when we had three inch line. At one time it went to three inch double jacketed rubber line as feed lines. In anything that looked good, you dropped the Smith valve with one three inch

* The Smith valve or Newark valve as it was known outside the city, was a large Y shaped aluminum valve with two spring-loaded clapper valves. It was developed by Newark Battalion Chief Robert Smith and allowed engine companies to change the hydrant connection from a 2 ½" outlet to a 4"outlet. In the days before large diameter hose, this enabled maximum use of the water from a hydrant.

and you dropped the two and a half too and stretched, which helped quite a bit. Then you could go in or do anything you wanted. In the Fourth Battalion, we used to use pre-connected deck guns off the tanks and really give it a shot. Then the guys could get in with hand lines while the driver put the feeds into their rigs.

When I was at Nine Engine we were using boxes on the side under the ladders to store inch and a half hose. They were made out of plywood and you'd have three lengths in there. You'd just put it on your shoulder and went with it, but most of the time you had to come off the back with most of it. You didn't wait. You grabbed it. In Nine we knew just how much we had. We just put it on our shoulders and took some off and waited for the next guy to grab the rest. We could stretch in very fast. There were a lot innovations and new hose, like the four inch hose that we use. When I first came on you had to take a hydrant. I don't care if you were a mile away from the fire; you had to take a hydrant, which was ridiculous. Sometimes it worked against you.

Denvir: (appointed 1959) We had pre-connected inch and a half when I came on. If you need two and a half, you'd take two and a half. Normally, you'd stretch inch and a half. Usually a couple of truckmen would go to the roof and the other two guys would go with the engine company. They would force entry and open the walls and the ceilings. But a lot of guys got over come. It was too thick. You had to take the mask.

Freda: (appointed 1959) If the hydrant was close enough to the fire, you would stop the pumper dead, hook it up to the hydrant, take the two and half inch line off, and stretch it by hand to the fire. Now, if you came upon a fire or you thought the stretch was too long to pull it by hand, then you would go to the fire building, drop the tip, and calculate, it's going to take me fourteen lengths to get to that hydrant beyond it and leave the tip at the scene with a couple of people or wrap it around something. Then you would drive the pumper and hook up to the hydrant.

The only time you wouldn't stretch from the hydrant is when what they called the Heffernan valve was already attached to it. The Heffernan valve was a four way valve that another pumper could hook up into and keep pumping into your line while they hooked up to the hydrant. There was one flaw to it. There was a stigma about it. Nobody wanted to use it. Nobody knew how to use it. Nobody wanted to know how to use it. It was like a computer to people today. They wouldn't go near it. There weren't too many companies that ever stopped and hooked it up. They would go by it like it was the plague. They would go around the corner. They would back up.

Now I saw one once and hooked up to it. You had to know which way to throw the valve. I hooked up and thought I was cool as a young kid. One of my first opportunities to pump and I pumped water in a circle. Out of the hydrant into the pumper and back into the hydrant. Around in a three sixty circle. I never wanted to use it again after that because people laughed at me for two weeks. So that was the end of me using the Heffernan valve. In fact, the Heffernan valve died out shortly after that because nobody would use it. But for the most part, the cardinal rule remained that you had to have your pumper at a hydrant.

Once the fire was knocked down, we had a connection then called the Mangor adaptor that you would put on the tip of your two and a half. Then you would hook an inch and a half line up into that and put that into the building.

In Twelve Engine that changed a little bit. The tactics changed because they had more fires. Fifteen Engine used a lot of two and a half inch hand lines inside the building. When I went to Twelve Engine, to the so called busy houses, you avoided a two and a half even if it was needed to cover exposures. Sometimes it was needed and you'd still see people using inch and a half lines. Everything changed. It was like joining a different fire department. The tactics changed. The hoses got smaller. I guess the more macho you got, the smaller the hose. You see a lot of these things are psychological believe it or not. Sissies use big hose for a lot of water. We macho men don't need big hose like that. We use the smaller hose because we're going to go in and attack this fire and we're going to wrestle with it and kill it.

Another interesting thing, when I was the captain in Twelve Engine, no matter what box we went on the booster was stretched to the front of the building. If we didn't have anything showing or no report of what was going on, the booster line was taken off the rig and put on the front porch of the house. If we didn't need it, rolled it up, that's a throwback to the days when you stretched a booster and then backed it up with a two and a half. All you're doing today is an extension of those tactics.

Charpentier: (appointed 1959) I would say the procedure of stretching inch and a half in with a mask on started when the younger men were made chief officers, with the likes of Chief Nolen, Chief Grehl, Chief Kinnear. In their group, it more or less changed to pre-connected inch and a half line, to everybody masking up on the way to a fire or before they got on the apparatus to go to a fire. It was a little more aggressive.

Where with the older chiefs, you had to wait and then hook up. Very few of them went for pre-connected lines and the small line. It wasn't until the mid-60s that almost everybody did wind up with pre-connected inch and a half hose. When the newer apparatus started to come in, that was when they had the Mattydales*. It was SOP then. At Six Engine, we used a two and half inch port with a wye on it. And we had two inch and a half pre-connected lines, which lied on top of the hose bed, which we later put into cradles we made ourselves. All we had to do was pull it off the top and then stretch it in. But the older chiefs wanted you to wait. You get there, then you hook your two and a half inch up or if you had inch and a half, and maybe reluctantly go in with it. Then you would mask up and everything. But when the newer younger chiefs, the World War II veterans were coming back, they had to go through the rank of captain. When they started making Battalion Chief and Deputy Chief; that's when there was a turn over. A lot of them brought back the ideas from the service during the World War. They put it into effect. We really were aggressive, real aggressive back then. Not that we weren't before, but it was what we had to work with. I know we had the Burrells in Six Engine. You'd come in in the morning and the Burrells would be hanging over the hose or the ladders. You'd have to take them off because this chief didn't want them out. He wanted them put into the boxes, lying on top of the apparatus.

Smith: (appointed 1959) If there's a working fire and you can see it or the driver gets a message and rings the bell to tell you on the back step you have something, you put the Burrell mask on. When you pulled up you could see you'll need either two and a half or inch and a half. If there's any way to get in, you would know that. By the time the other rigs pulled up, the two guys had the inch and a half off and they were going into the building. What we

---

* A Mattydale or cross lay spans the width of a fire engine and allows firefighters to stretch hose from the side of the rig.

did was pull an extra length or two off and let it lay in the street so you could maneuver inside the building.

The driver would immediately hook up and give you the tank. But in the meantime, before that was even done, he had a water supply because your engine took the hydrant, stretched a line down, and hooked up to the wagon. If he needed another one, he'd run up to the wagon, take hose off their hydrant side, run back to the engine, hook it up, and put that in. He could do it with a third line if he needed it. If it were a big enough job, he'd do it with a third line. That's if you were first or second due.

Where I was there were three two-piece companies. So the other companies coming in could take their hose off the rigs in front of the building. It was a mechanical process. You learned after a while just by simply looking at it, what you were going to use. The captain didn't have to run off and say, "You do this. You do this. You do this."

If I was riding the pipe side of the wagon with the inch and a half and I saw a building fire I would just take the line and run into the building. They would charge the line. In the meantime, the guy next to me would have the mask on. He would come in and take the line. Then I would come back out and get my mask and go in, but the line was in there. It was working instantaneously. That was the idea of it.

Dunn: (appointed 1959) Our basic tactics were to pull up in front of the building. Then the captain and one or two men would stretch the pre-connected line and attack the fire. What you won't see going on today that we did is the driver would go get water. Today the driver assists the guy with the line because usually there's only one fireman. He will assist in getting the line stretched, so he can't go get water. He's relying on the second due engine company or the third due engine company to get water.

Twenty years ago it was your job to go get the water. As soon as that line was being stretched, your job was to put your fed line on your shoulder, if you didn't get a hydrant coming in, and start back stretching. If a company came along, fine. You'd have your line there. He could pump to you. But that evolution has died out because of manpower.

The other change you see as far as effectiveness is if you ride a truck company one and two and they're first on the scene. The first law of the fire department is to go rescue people. Make a search, but then we don't get any ventilation. So, our truck companies are really stretched with this limited manpower to what function you want them to do. If the chief is not there first, they do whatever function they perceive to be important.

It's much different riding in with a truck company or two truck companies that have one officer and two men, than it was riding in with two truck companies with one and four. We used to try to maintain them at one and four because we might throw ground ladders up. When you did go to a fire, you could get people to the roof and get good roof ventilation and still have forcible entry and an attack team going into the building. Today you are just spreading yourself so thin. The only thing helping us is we're not getting the good fires.

Tactics haven't really changed. Tactics in the 1930's for example are the same tactics we're using today. Rescue, confine, control, and extinguish your fires. We use different strategies to accomplish it sometimes, but basically the change isn't there. The change that's coming in the fire service that's happening in Newark is private fire protection. You don't have fires on Doremus Avenue anymore. I can't tell you the last time I've been to a fire on Doremus Avenue. When I was a kid living Down Neck, you would have a fire on Doremus Avenue once a week. Something would blow up and the fire department would come and throw a ton of water and flush everything into the Passaic River. A week later there would be a guy there laying brick. Today with the private fire suppression systems that are installed, the foam systems, the heat detector systems, the automatic water flow systems, and the insurance industry enforcing their own requirements, the fire problem in that area has been reduced. There's always going to be the one that blows up every now and then, but overall the safety is built into the system.

But the tactics basically have not changed in my mind over the years. We've changed responses; we have changed our equipment; we have changed our manpower; but the basic underlying tactic has really stayed the same.

Harris: (appointed 1961) When I came into the job, we went strictly inside to fight. It wasn't surround and drown. We used to fight to get upstairs to the fire. You went over guys. You get in, put the fire out, and go back. That's what we always thought we had to do. Save as much property as possible. Save lives and get out. And camaraderie, when you went to a fire whether you were black or you were white, you fought a fire. You went in that building. You fought that fire. You shook the guys in. You drank out of the same coffee cup afterwards. You shared water together. You shared your mask together and then you came back to the firehouse. With us it was Twenty Engine, Six Engine, Twelve Engine, and Ten Engine. We fought constantly. Who was first due?

Twenty Engine was a two piece company. Seventeen was a two piece company at that time. We never lacked for water. We never lacked for manpower. You always had something. You were always backing up. You brought your own water and when you hit that building; the tip man and the captain were in there. That second man was backing him up and then you relieved. The guy didn't get killed in there. We always did this, but now it's to the point where the Chief's got to call in a second alarm or another nine to relieve the guys. We did it ourselves at the fire. If your guy was in there, you got your guy out. You grabbed him. "Let's get out of here." The minute he'd start coughing you knew that little all purpose mask was used up. "Let's get out of here." And you'd just follow your line and go out. If you stood in the doorway, we'd run you over. We're going up those stairs or getting into that first floor. We didn't allow you to do that. We just had that thing about us. Maybe it was that stupid macho whatever you want to call it. But this is what we did. This is what we did and you fought fires. You went in. You put the fire out.

Haran: (appointed 1961) At Salvage when the alarm came in, which Salvage unit responded would depend on what section of the city the alarm was in. Salvage Two caught mostly one and four boxes and some three boxes. I was in Salvage One. We caught three boxes, five boxes, and most of the two boxes down on Frelinghuysen Avenue. We were protecting the property during the fire.

When the alarm came in there were four engines companies, two truck companies, a Battalion Chief, Deputy Chief, the Rescue Squad, and the Salvage Corps. The Salvage Corps also went. Our primary thing was to try and protect the furniture and people's goods in the home. A lot of times we went out to Frelinghuysen Avenue which is predominantly a manufacturing area, big factories down there that manufacture products. They're all sprinkled. They had systems in all those buildings. During the winter time we used to go out all hours of the night and day, especially when the weather got cold. We used to have cracked sprinkler heads and cracked pipes. We went on them. We used to replace the sprinkler heads and we billed them. The city used to send them a bill to repair that. We used to pump out cellars. First aid cases, knifing, shootings, stabbings, drug overdoses, we did a multitude of things. But the primary thing was responding to a fire and throwing salvage covers and protecting the property on the floor below.

A lot of times some of the fires were so big that Salvage One used to call Salvage Two to give them a hand. Salvage Two used to call Salvage One. One in particular I can remember, the old Newark Slip Factory on High Street right on Raymond Boulevard where Raymond Boulevard passes underneath. We had a fire in there one night during the winter. The sprinkler system went off and the alarm never sounded. As a result the building was flooded. There was a fire that set a lot of heads off and the building was flooded. Captain Schimpf called Salvage One up to give him a hand. We had to remove the water in that building. It was an occupied building. It was mostly clothing in there and we did what we called shooting the water out of the building. There were elevators in there. We rolled salvage covers down the stairs one over the other to shoot the water out like you would shoot coal down into a coal chute. We had squeegees and we pushed the water from one side of the building to the other side of the building where the staircases were. We'd make these chutes and there'd be dams to control the flow of the water. I saw him do that and even though it shows pictures in the old Oklahomas and different books, this was the first time I really had ever done that. It was interesting. Not only that, we removed the toilets in the bathrooms. By removing the toilets we had a big four inch opening there where all the water went down into the sewer system that way.

Then when we got down into the basement, we had two, three feet of water down in there. We cracked the sewage pipes with sledge hammers.

Now, it sounds like we're doing damage, but by far we're reducing the water damage that's going to occur to the building. After the water all goes, you just replace the section of pipe. Then we put the toilet back on.

Well, those things stuck with me over the years. They were things that I had learned in Salvage and they were some of the things we did in Salvage. Just not too long ago, maybe six or seven years ago, we had a fire on South Orange Avenue. It was a delicatessen, butcher type of store. The fire burned in the cellar. The refrigeration, which is heavy by itself, came down through the floor and we had four, five feet of water in the basement. I had young guys.

Today it's slower than it was years ago. You don't run into the same situations. You don't get as much experience. We went up there and we went down the basement. I said, "How are we going to do this. So, I just felt around the wall. I watched where the sewer pipe came down through the building and I remembered this from thirty-eight years ago. There was a sewer pipe right there, right up against the wall. I told John, one of the fellows that works with me, I said, "Crack that pipe open. Break that pipe there, right there where it comes up, about eight inches off the floor." He says, "Cap, what's that going to do?" I said, "That's what we're going to do. That's how we're going to relieve this place of the water." So, we broke the pipe off and then we took a flat milk carton with the holes in it and we put it over the opening like a strainer. In a couple of hours all the water had drained out of the basement. It was cool. John said, "I learned something today." I learned from Schimpf thirty years ago. That type of thing still comes into play today. Removing the toilets which a lot of guys wouldn't think of, I learned that from an old guy, Captain Schimpf at that time. They were all good things. That was all new to me at that time. I remembered those things over the years.

In Salvage, when it was a multiple alarm, surround and drown type of fire. Then it's just like a truck company. What does a truck company do when it's a surround and drown type thing? They go to an engine company. They pull off a two and a half and they stand outside and hit it. Well, that's what we did. We were manpower out there. Obviously, there was no salvage work to be done. We worked sometimes as a secondary unit. We could go in, maybe, at a fire not of the magnitude of a surround and drown type thing. Because a surround and drown type the thing is fully involved. You're just containing it from the exposure. But there have been times when the fire was severe enough where you weren't going to save anything, but now you're going to go in as a secondary rescue unit. So, you work in conjunction with the Rescue Squad searching, search and rescue.

Cahill: (appointed 1963) The Second Division used two and a half inside a building, where the First Division would use inch and a half, functioning very well with it. Down Neck they believed in big water. Finally, they got to the point where you could stop, at least break it down in the hallway to inch and a half, then finally just inch and a half. But primarily down here it was big water that's what the chiefs would call for. Of course you had one and four, but even at that it was difficult into a two or three story frame, but if you didn't come in with two and a half you were in trouble.

We used a lot of boosters depending on what you had. It would vary. If you had a smoke condition, you used a two and a half. If it's nothing showing or a mattress fire or something like that, you used a booster. We had no in-between, where up on the hill they used the inch and a half.

Highsmith: (appointed 1963) Nineteen Engine wasn't that busy, but most of our runs were work. It was a signal five, three oh eight, three oh nine, signal eleven.* Most of them were work and we had a lot out in the airport, where the airport parking lot is now. Off Route One and Nine, a lot of bus fires out there where the Radisson Hotel is now. We had a lot of brush fires out there and those are the hardest things to fight because we had no water. We had to go in there with brooms and try to beat them out because the train companies never did put hydrants in their yards, so we had to beat them out or try and let them burn out. You know, surround them. It was rough.

We were in the Second Battalion, so we didn't get up to the Fourth Battalion too much to fight fires because you had the big guns like Twelve Engine. Ten Engine would come from the Second Battalion, shooting up there. You had Six Engine. You had Twenty Engine. These guys would put out a fire in no time. One thing about then and now, it took less firefighters and less equipment to put out large fires. We held our multiple alarms down to a minimum. Those guys took pride in that, the big guys up there on the hill. They took pride in knocking a fire down, holding it to themselves. They didn't want anybody to think, "Oh well, they let it get out of hand."

I worked on the fourth tour and they called us the parking lot tour. Because every time we got something they said it burned down to the ground. When I went down to Ten Engine on a detail and rode up on the hill I saw the way they fought fires was a little faster paced than I guess we did it down in the Second Battalion. The guys, they went right in there, right at the seat of the fire. The first due company did their job, the second due company did theirs. It was like that throughout the fire department. The first due company knew what they had to do. They got to a building. They

---

* Signal five is a single company response, a three oh eight includes an engine, a truck and a battalion chief, a three oh nine includes two engines, a truck, and a battalion chief, and a signal eleven commits an entire assignment typically consisting of four engines, two trucks, a battalion chief, a deputy chief, and the rescue squad.

go in and attack it. If it was a building with standpipes, the second due company had to come and hook up to the standpipe. Everybody did their job and when the big guys came, sometimes they'd run over you if you don't get out of their way, but it was a lot of fun. If there was any difference in firefighting between different battalions, different deputy divisions, it was all for the better. It was just a lot of competition. That's all it was.

Butler: (appointed 1963) When I came on everybody was well programmed. It was an automatic that the second and probably the third due engine companies brought water. First due engine was free to roam sort of speak. At the fire building they were just a little past the fire building because the SOP at that time that was really enforced was to leave room in front of the building for the aerial company, the truck company. They had to raise their aerial for any rescues or ventilation purposes. They always had the room in front of the building to operate. But you had a situation I'd say probably in the early '70s where some real rivalries with engine companies were out there. In the center city you had Six, Twelve, Twenty, Seven, Eleven, even Four Engine, they had a real rivalry where they tried to beat each other into the box and steal a fire.

With the truck company, quite often I'd be up on somebody's front lawn because I wanted to get to the building next to them. It didn't really concern me that "Oh, I'm riding on somebody's grass and I'm going to put a hole in their lawn or something." All that can be dug up. I'm trying to get to a house and ventilate it in order to be able to let the guys underneath get a break. I didn't care, within reason; I didn't really care what I ran over. I banged down fences more than once, cyclone fences, just hit it right at the corner post and took it down so I can get close enough so the ladder would be affective, away from trees or wires or something. But I had that ladder to a point where I could really do almost anything with it.

I always look for a second way to get to a fire, especially if I were second due truck company. Trying to figure how the other truck company is going to get to that street and I want to come in a different way. Especially, in Vailsburg because you're dealing with Twelve Truck there and that was part of our second due area. I'd cut up through East Orange because I knew Twelve Truck would be facing in from South Orange Avenue. I'd cut up through East Orange and come out Tremont Avenue to the scene and come towards it from the other direction. Quite often we were successful in raising our aerial ladder where Twelve Truck was stuck with the wires, trees, or whatever.

Cody: (appointed 1964) When I came on we had pre-connected inch and a half that we would stretch into a building, first due, and work off the booster tank. That's an SOP. That's the way we did it. The engine we had at Four Engine had three hundred gallons. But we had spare engines with a hundred and fifty gallons. You had to work real quick to get in because you were out of water real fast. You had to be very careful about how far you went. Even the three hundred gallons, you can knock down a lot of fire with three hundred gallons, but it goes pretty quick.

As a Battalion Chief you just position yourself at a command post in front of the building. You try to ascertain where the fire is, if there's a life hazard involved, and how you're going to deploy your companies as they arrive. Of course, if there's a life hazard, you're going to commit everyone to rescue. If there's a fire on the first floor and there are people on the second floor, you're still going to commit to the fire because by putting out the fire, you're more or less rescuing the people upstairs. You're getting a line between the fire and the people. You get ventilation. If there's no life hazard, your truck is going to do your ventilation for you. It's easier access for the engine to get into the fire and work up to the fire without all that smoke build up and heat buildup. Give the heat and smoke an avenue of escape.

Garrity: (appointed 1964) Well, it depended on what you were doing. If you had a job and you were driving or tillering the truck, you were a roof man. The driver would start putting up the aerial. We used to manually put out outriggers. The tillerman would start the outriggers. We didn't have a tiller cab that had to come off the ladder. I think we were the first truck that had a tiller cab behind the ladder. That guy would pull out the outriggers, screw them down to the ground, getting the building side first. Then the driver would start putting the aerial ladder up. Then the two guys would go to the roof, do whatever venting had to be done, and then you'd come back inside. If we were one and four, the other two guys went with the captain inside; did the forcible entry, the search and the ventilation from inside, overhaul and that kind of thing. That's the way the company was basically worked. The engine would stretch in the front door with your inch and a half. The guys would go up and pull the ceilings. The biggest change I think we got was saws. We started with chain saws on the roof and they never worked right. Then eventually we got the circular saws.

Knight: (appointed 1964) I got out of the truck company in 1980. Primarily, when I got out of the truck company, we were still doing basic truck work. You had your roof ventilation. That was the name of the game. You had to get it opened and get it ventilated or else the guys with the lines couldn't get in. They knew that if they had to make the second or the third floor, if that roof wasn't opened they were going to have problems getting up there. Basic truck work was enter, search, ventilate, and overhaul. If you were needed for rescues, that's what you were there for, for the rescues. Primary was life. If there was no life hazard involved, then your next job was property, extinguishing. Today they have bigger rigs, bigger truck companies. They did away with all the tiller truck companies in the city of Newark, which I think was a farce. I believe in the city of Newark, any of these big cities, you need truck companies that have a tillerman because you have streets in the city that you can't get down with these big rigs, these rear mounts. With a tractor driven aerial ladder with a tillerman, you could get down these streets. You could jockey into position in tight spots. With these new rigs you can't. This is modern firefighting. We didn't have that back then.

If you had to use a ladder pipe, you had to stretch hose up a ladder to use your ladder pipe. Now the ladder pipes are pre-connected right to the aerial. All they do is hook into an inlet in the back of the apparatus and there you go. Everything's hydraulic. Everything's electronic. We didn't have that. You had to go up and work these ladder pipes by hand. You had to use ropes. They had halyards to move them up and down. If you wanted to change a pattern, you had to go up, send a man up the aerial to change the pattern of the stream. Nowadays you don't do that. Nowadays everything is hydraulic. You just push buttons. It changes the pattern, changes the stream. I think truck work has come a long way. There are still a lot of things that can be done. Primarily the truck companies get their work done. They have no qualms with the truck companies they have. The guys do a good job.

Wargo: (appointed 1964) There was a difference in tactics between fires in three story frames and fighting fires in chemical factories even then, even without haz-mat. People would stand back and take a look at what you have. You went to certain chemical places out on inspection, so you knew what they handled in there. You had to be careful when you went in. Of course the equipment was bigger. You used a lot of heavy streams and you used a lot of two and a half inch hose. You would take it inside. You would take it right into the guts of the building and operate because it was big volumes of water, big open areas and then you would wye off. That's what you had most of the time.

After I was promoted, I went to a company where most of the work was in dwellings with inch and half. Grab a line and go in with it that way. We did have a couple of places on Orchard Street. In fact we were there quite a few times. That became like a drill. Deck gun, get in, first due company give it a shot with the tank while we're hooking up. Then take the inch and half and go in and work. We had a little bit of everything. It was really pretty good. I liked it a lot.

McGovern: (appointed 1968) Mostly in the Squad we did truck work. It was, "Chief, what do you want?" Rescue wasn't really just searching. The chief would say get the roof, take a line here. You never knew what you were going to do. It was totally foreign compared to what I did in Twenty-seven. You learned all aspects of firefighting. Whoever was driving was the outside guy. He would set up a first aid station. We each did that for a month. You'd take turns monthly driving, but during that month you're standing in front. You get to see the system work. Just by standing there, being able to observe it all as opposed to running into the building and not seeing anything. So, it's a good learning tool just doing it that way; a good opportunity to learn. I tried to absorb all I could. Plus, I always worked with good people. They were more than willing to help you.

Finucan: (appointed 1969) We're still an interior firefighting outfit. Guys still are highly motivated in busy companies. The people who want to be, still like to go to fires, still give a hundred percent, most of them, even though they're one and two or one and three. Strangely enough, the firefighter is a funny breed. Most of the guys like their job and they do their job. They enjoy the fire end of it.

Cosby: (appointed 1969) Well, it was basically the first due engine would take the front of the building and the second due engine would feed the first due engine. I think it was the same as it is today. If the fire is inside the building, you would stretch; at that time when I came on it was inch and a half hose. You would stretch inch and a half hose inside to attack the fire if the fire was confined to the inside of the building. But if the house was fully involved or it had spread to the outside, you would basically use the big line, two and a half inch, to more or less knock it down so you could go inside. I think that's basically what they do today.

Pianka: (appointed 1970) When you pulled up and you had a fire, you jumped off the back, one guy would grab the inch and a half, especially if we were first due, and he would take it inside, right inside the house. He would start taking the tip in as the rest of us would mask up. So, let's say we were one and four. He's in there with the tip. We could come right up there, take the tip. He would come back, either stay back and flake out the line or go get his mask.

Every fire is different. Sometimes the line was dry. He would just give it to one of the guys, come back. Sometimes the guy wouldn't want to give it up. He'd shout out at you. I know I did that a couple of times. Water was coming anyway, so I would just work it a little bit until I couldn't do any more, "Here, you take it now." I'd go back down and get my mask. Then again, like I said, when we were a full compliment, sometimes we would take two lines. Either two lines inside or one line would go around the back. That was the benefit of riding heavy.

In the trucks, the SOPs really haven't changed dramatically. It's the same. Two guys go to the roof, other guys go inside. You work as a team. On the engine it's still the same thing depending if you're first due or second due. Everybody has their own assigned jobs. The driver is supposed to try to get water if he doesn't have a feed line already. The other guys stretch either one or two lines. They haven't changed dramatically there.

We always worked off the tank. I don't know if it was because I was with Bobby Dunbar and that was the way Bobby worked. There were times when I remember guys wouldn't give you tank water and they were senior men. Because that's just not the way they did it. They wouldn't do anything until they got water from a hydrant, not at Six Engine, other companies. I mean, you'd run into Down Neck companies. That wasn't that often and a lot of times you had to tell people, "Hey, give me your tank. What are you waiting for?" We worked off the tank a lot. That's why I said one of the great innovations now is a booster tank with seven hundred fifty gallons of water. That's tremendous. That's a lot to go in with a hand line. Your inch and three quarter, it gives you a good five minutes, which gives you plenty of time to get a chunk of that fire and get a supply.

McDonnell: (appointed 1970) The one thing was they attacked. The method of firefighting was basically interior attack. There were a lot of guys. There were a lot of lines stretched. If you didn't get water, then it was holy hell. If a company came to the fire and didn't get water, after the fire the chief would say, "Lay two." If you were in an engine company, you got a hydrant. You didn't come into the fire without water. That was the attitude. The attitude was you're going to do this job. That was basically the attitude that almost everybody had. If you didn't want to do it, you certainly didn't say it. You'd be out in the yard. They'd be beating the shit out of you. That was pretty much it. They had that attitude to get in there. When you went to a fire with tons of lines and you got there late, you weren't getting anything. I can remember being on the stairs and there'd be fifteen, twenty guys on the stairs. You were on the bottom. That was their attitude, get in, get in. It was the attitude of busy companies.

Rivalries were intense. Engine companies would get into fist fights trying to get the first water on the fire. Not so much with the truck companies. You couldn't do anything really. There was a rivalry to get the roof, to get in first and get the roof or even to get to the alarm location faster. To beat somebody to the alarm, they used to do that. Try to get the hell in there as fast as they could. Try to get there before the other companies. They used to do that, drive like maniacs and to get the roof. "We got their roof." They did have that. They could beat the other guy to the roof. Sometimes they'd be coming in at the same time.

It wasn't so much at One Truck because they had the snorkel and there were a ton of times when it was really hard to get that thing up. Sometimes it had like a mind, it could think because it would work all day. When we'd go to a fire it wouldn't go up. You couldn't get the damn thing to work. It was like, ah. That was different because a lot of times we went to fires and you'd use that if they wanted big water.

When I was promoted I pretty much kept what it was as a fireman. It was pretty much standard in the truck company. The driver and the tillerman went to the roof. The captain and the side men went inside or if they needed ground ladders or whatever. The basic operations stayed the same. In the city there was a little less attack by this time, by the late 70's. A little less of attack, attack, attack and go inside all the time. It was a little more of big water and outside lines.

My thing is it's the most important thing. Guys, "You got to have balls." I always felt like you needed balls. You needed brains. And you needed to be willing to do it. Other guys who say, "Well, he's afraid," if guys weren't enthusiastic about going to fires. I always felt they didn't want to do it. I'm afraid. If you're not afraid in a fire, you're a nut, something's wrong with you. You should be. You need that spirit. You need that feeling. When I came on it was the company spirit, the rivalry. We want to be better than them. We all stick together. You need that to do this job. You can't pay somebody to risk their life. It has to be a conscious decision that person makes. It's not, "If you give me a raise I'll run in there harder or something." That's not the way it works. Guys did it, do it because they have a feeling that it's something worthwhile. And that you should do it.

T. Grehl: (appointed 1971) On a truck, the driver and the tillerman took the roof. Other than if it's a life hazard, everything goes by the wayside and you do what you have to do. But a working fire with everybody out of it or a regular building structure, the driver and tillerman took the roof. The captain and one or two of his men, depending on the balance, would take the captain's tool and or hooks and axes and go inside with forcible entry, ventilate, take out the windows, and do what they had to do. SOPs were always the driver and the tillerman went to the roof. That was it, on the first due company. The second due company, it kind of varies, but it was basically the same concept that they would go inside. If they weren't needed inside, the other driver and the tiller would go up to the roof also to help, to assist the first truck. But other than that, if there was no heavy thing everybody would just go inside.

Ryan: (appointed 1973) The main thing is if you were the driver of the first due engine, figure out where the first due truck is coming from. Leave them enough room to get to the front of the building so they can get the roof, which makes your job dramatically easier. First due engine gets a line in and gets command of the stairway. If the fire was on the first floor, move in and get it. If it was upstairs, again take command of the stairway in case there are people to get out, you can get them out. Second due engine would usually go to the floor below unless you weren't moving in. Again there was great competition to get to the fire. If you were too slow, somebody was right up your butt. So, you liked to get in there.

Truck company first due, aerial to the roof, open the roof. Wires a problem? Yes. I think they were easier under certain circumstances, but you always had wires. When I first drove, we had an American LaFrance rear mount at Eleven Truck. I found it to be a lot easier to spot the ladder because from where you looked you could see whether there was a hole through the wires to get to the roof or through the trees or whatever. You could visualize where it was going to go. Whereas with a tractor trailer job, the ladder was bedded to the back and you had to do a full swing and take a lot of time to get it around. So the rear mounts worked out much better. First due truck company, two men went to the roof, two men inside opening up.

First due engine usually rode free, was able to run free into the fire, but again keep the truck in mind, because they can't bend the ladder. If you're coming in after first due and you knew the water mains, you come in so you could stretch from a large main. Knowing the mains is something that took a while. At the time you had fellows who were steady drivers and it was beneficial because of the mains. Guys actually knew the fire main system. You had to know where there were good hydrant runs and stretch in from that hydrant. Sometimes it meant going around the block and coming in from the opposite direction. You have horrible hydrants here. Like on Sussex Avenue, it had a high pressure hydrant main that ran down Sussex Avenue. So if I was going to go that way, I'd go down Sussex and bring it in with me.

As companies were put out of service around us, we actually got into the habit of not riding free into a fire. We would always stretch a feed in, because of the time delay. There was a time when Seven Engine, Twenty Engine, and Two Engine went out of service. There was nobody to bring you water if you were falling into that particular configuration of alarm assignment. They were pretty close to each other. So, if we were going down Central Avenue to a fire you had to figure where to get water. You only had Four Engine coming up and the other people were at a distance.

The thinking process was really important. If you stop and think now, how many guys know where the good water mains are? That I don't know, but we had guys who knew. These were the World War II vets, who had been around for a long time. "Get that hydrant over there. I know that one works good." Or "Bring it down the avenues. Take it off an avenue. You had a better shot than one in the middle of the block or, God forbid, one on a dead end street." But if that's all you have, that's all you work with.

Langenbach: (appointed 1973) Truck, as much as I kidded them after I got into the engine, is a pretty important job, the ventilation, not even the rescue part of it, just the ventilation, forcible entry. Get the guys with the lines into the building to do their jobs. Get the ceilings down for them. I think it's something that people aren't doing the way it used to be done. I don't think it's getting the attention it should get. It's hard work. Truck work is hard work. If you do it right, it's really hard. I mean you're really going to work. But it's one of those jobs. If you don't want to do it, it's not hard not to do it. We used to kid the guys who used to be in the closet with the hook and then come up after everything is done. Interesting stuff, it's not for everybody because you have to work by yourself. That's a difficult thing for a lot of people. You have to be able to work on your own, independent of anybody. You're not going to have a boss around like you do with the engine. I like the engine work better. I liked putting the fire out. I don't like looking for the fire, pulling ceilings. Get in there and knock it down. So I enjoyed engine work a lot more, especially as a captain.

When I was at Five Truck, we still had the tiller, so the driver and the tillerman got the roof; that was their job, top ventilation. Then the sidemen and the captain would go inside and do forcible entry, whatever. Then you would get back together again. When guys were done with the roof, they would come inside and do overhaul or ventilation or whatever. It was pretty organized. It was organized chaos, but it was organized. Everybody knew; that was the nice thing about having the driver and the tillerman go to the roof. They knew exactly what they were going to do and they worked as a team. It was funny because when I got to Five Truck, I could tiller, so I tillered in the summer when it was hot and Quirk tillered in the winter when it was cold because we had just gotten that sliding cab with the little heater in it.

Luxton: (appointed 1973) The first due engine was able to run free. If you saw a hydrant and it wasn't that inconvenient, you dropped a line and stretched in. Most of the time, Six Engine didn't do that. We had a five

---

hundred gallon booster tank and we just went to work on it. You stretched in. When we were one and five we could take three lines in, most of time it was two. The captain would be between two guys who had two lines. You'd take the first and second floor. You threw a mask on before you went in. Sometimes you didn't use it and you'd just let it hang there. When it got too hot and smoky you'd take a couple of breaths of air and keep going, idiots that we were. Another one of the procedures we used to do on some of these vacant and abandoned buildings. We'd dump the deck gun right off our tank and knock down the main body of fire. Then you could basically walk right up the stairs with an inch and a half. We were able to do that quite a bit.

It was up to the driver to get some water. The second due engine usually would stretch in and make sure you had water. You would just go to work on the fire. Five Truck was good. Nine Truck was good, Eleven. We had Three Truck then too. Teddy DeSordi was there. They follow you in and open up and do what they had to do.

Pignato: (appointed 1974) Since I worked without a captain for the first few years on the job, my SOP was if I was driving or tillering, I went to the roof. There was competition between us, Seven Truck, and Three Truck. You get in front of the building. If you get the engine companies out of the damn way, so you can get in front of the building, you go to the roof. You do all the top ventilation. We used to get a lot of two and a half story frames in the North Newark area. Instead of going crazy with the aerial ladder and trying to get it up on the peak through trees and everything else, Harry Tokanos and I would just grab a thirty foot straight, run it to the back yard, and ladder it that way. We'd be on the roof before everybody else had their outriggers out. That was a little thing we did by ourselves, with a ground ladder we'd get it up there just as fast.

Langevin: (appointed 1974) When I came on the job in '74, the typical Newark evolution of first due engine pulling up stretching in inch and a half, first due truck getting the roof, and everybody else kind of working off of what was already in place. With the two-piece engine companies, the wagon stretched down the street. The pumper took the hydrant. The truck went to the roof for ventilation and overhauling and everything else like that. Second, third due engines usually came in from the opposite way, so does the truck. But sometimes you got people and apparatus just lined up and down the street. You needed a second ladder and you couldn't get it anywhere near the building. But that's the typical big city and small streets thing. Sometimes it couldn't be helped.

I had volunteered in another town before I came to Newark. It was a decent department, but most volunteer outfits fight fires differently than we do here in Newark because we pride ourselves on being an interior fire department. A lot of volunteer fire departments just pour water in from the outside. I was impressed we can take the bull by the horns as it were and charge right in through the front door.

Perdon: (appointed 1974) The first truck company I was in when I first came on the job, SOPs were actually an embarrassment. There were times where the SOP was to do as little as possible. You had your standing orders because you had to have them, ventilation and everything. One of the first fires I went to, we went to the roof. We opened up everything on the roof, but it's still one of those things. I've seen the captain do strange things. It was like do as little as possible. I would walk away and I would get in trouble eventually. But I would help people with lines and stuff like that. "What are you doing?" We caught a job, a big factory on Johnson Street around the corner from Fourteen Engine. We put up two ground ladders and I'm saying, "Wow, we're actually going to do some serious work here." He put the ground ladder up here and then I saw another one was over here, two ways up, two ways down, smart move. Followed him. He went up this one, walked across the roof, down that one, and sat on a bumper. I just went and helped with some lines up there. I got in all kinds of trouble. But I was so embarrassed when I saw that. That was standard unfortunately.

At Seventeen Engine we had SOPs. They were really the same as we do today. It was you get there first due. You stretch a line. You go right to the fire. Your driver is doing his hook up. You're not involved in that. Your function is to get that line, get the water on the fire. Same as it is now. No different.

Bisogna: (appointed 1974) Twenty Engine was in the center of the city, so we would stretch one or two lines in as long as we had enough guys. I guess when I first got on; they would grab Six Engine's lines and try to pull these guys down the stairs. Besides racing each other to the fire, they would actually fight on the stairs to get a line on the fire. These guys were pretty much animal. Attack, attack, attack, they just would charge in. I was only there a year and a half and I didn't do that much driving there. They were remiss. They didn't want to bring water. They just wanted to go put water on the fire. But we did have two pieces, so we did stretch a lot of hose. I remember hooking up and running down the block with it. And it just seemed like just get the water to the fire. SOPs, like I said, we were busy. You didn't have to train about it because you kept doing it over and over and over again.

At Five Truck, we went to a lot of fires, opened a lot of roofs. Thank God most of them were flat. That made it easy. They were all three story frames and hardily any peaked roofs. In fact, I think I remember being on one peaked roof that was on fire. Peaked roofs are tougher. That's my opinion. A lot of times you put a ladder up and you work off the side of a ladder. You can only get a small hole. Where, you get a flat roof I can cut three holes in it and you think I'm a hero. Look at all the holes I made up here. I always thought that was one of the toughest jobs, going up on a roof, especially a peak roof. Flat roofs are pretty easy. Hard work, but then you get the break after. You get to take in the view. The poor guy making the third floor, he doesn't have a chance to look around, see the lights of New York.

Ricca: (appointed 1974) When I came on the job, the first due engine ran free and operated off the tank but hoping that the second due engine brought water in because they were fighting with the first due engine to see who got the first water on the fire. I heard of the Twenty Engine days of putting the hose between the banisters; I never saw it. But I have seen guys not lighten up, they'd lighten up their line to make it past the first due company. Not to make the first due company look bad. Just to get the fire. That's all it came down to. It was never meant to skunk somebody and say, "Well, we got it." It was just, "We put the fire out." That was it. There was so much pride back then. It was unbelievable. And unsung heroes, guys like Joe Lefchak, Shelly Smith, guys who worked until they were exhausted and then worked some more. Made rescues and never even thought about commendation or citation. They just did it to do it. Joe Lefchak had to save more firemen's kids on the job than anybody

Ray Stoffers is an exceptional, exceptional fireman. Very smart, I went to high school with Raymond and for some reason we just worked very, very well together. It was never like we both grabbed the saw. Whatever he grabbed, I grabbed the opposite. If he was tillering, I had the ladder going up as he was clearing the cage on the old truck. We never spoke a word to each other. We just knew what each other was doing. When Tommy came, his most important statement was, "I want the roof ventilated." And he never liked us touching an uninvolved house. He wouldn't want us to go to an uninvolved and jump to the involved one to cut the hole. He wanted us to keep off of the people's houses that were intact. Calvetti's main ladder was a thirty-five. He had us carry that with us. If we were going to the back, he had us carry that with us just in case you needed it.

Gesualdo: (appointed 1977) I can remember the SOP here was first due, take your line in. The way we use to work it was whatever side the fire was on, that's the person who grabbed the tip and then you went in pretty much without your breathing apparatus, which probably wasn't a wise thing to do. But I know that our practice here on Twenty-nine on the fourth tour was take the line in, get the water started, then your backup would bring your breathing apparatus in for you. He would have his on; take over the tip while you put yours on. And that was SOP. Find the seat of the fire. Get your line in there if you were first due, second due.

I very rarely drove because at the time we had a steady driver here. It wasn't a good practice, but I knew it coming in so I accepted it. If you were driving make sure your crew had water. If you're second due make sure you supplied water. Pretty much it was just go all out and knock the fire down. Get inside and knock the fire down and take up your hose. It wasn't too complicated. It was pretty straight forward. It's a little more structured now with the incident command system and you have to be a little more careful with your respective gear and things like that.

Chapter Two: On the Job 1942 to 1966

Fredette: There was the urn explosion over in Kearny around the end of 1942, beginning of 1943. We went over to Kearny on that. They had a lot of companies from Newark. It was a big four-story brick building. They were making some kind of powder or substance for camouflage nets and it exploded. It took this four-story building right down in a heap. I was in Nine Engine. The explosion occurred just at the change of shifts. We were up from Standard Oil down along the Passaic River and thought it was Standard Oil. We went right down there. Then we looked over across the river and saw it was over in Kearny, so we went back to quarters. The operator picked up and said respond to this explosion. We went there.

The two fireboats had come up originally on the explosion thinking it was Standard Oil. It was a good thing they did because that was really the only way of getting water. There were six outlets on each boat. That meant we could get twelve lines off. These two fire boats were the only ones who had the water. Down there along the Passaic River, all those hydrants were dead. One by one they kept bringing more companies from Newark. They brought in Ten Engine's hose wagon. They brought in Four Engine and Thirteen Engine. They must have stripped the city of thirty percent or thirty-five percent of all the companies. We stayed there a couple of days.

*   *   *   *   *

I was only on a couple of weeks when we had Reiss' Lumber on Crane and Webster. That was a four-alarm fire. The company started off making windows sashes and doorframes. Then it kept on expanding. It became a lumber company up in that area. That was a Nine Engine job.

*   *   *   *   *

We had a job on Prospect Place up in North Newark. The fire was on one side of the fireplace in the living room. We had to stay outside with the hose until they rolled up the rugs, so we could come in with our dirty boots to put out the fire alongside the fireplace. The Chief ordered us to stay outside because those rugs were worth maybe a hundred thousand dollars in this big, beautiful home on Prospect Place. That was the only fire where we had to wait until they rolled up the rugs and took the pictures off the walls before we put water on it.

*   *   *   *   *

There was a fire on Court and Mercer and a captain wanted to put Teddy Smith and me on charges because we wouldn't give up a line. It was up in a little cockloft and he wanted the Squad to take the line because they had masks and we didn't have any. At Six Engine, you never gave up your line to anybody, especially the Squad. The Chief talked him out of it. He said, "I want you to put these two guys on charges." The Chief said, "For what?" He said, "I ordered them to give me their line. They wouldn't give me their line." The Chief said, "I'd like to have more men like that."

We lost two people there. They were sleeping in a room in an attic that was about three feet high from the floor to the roof. They were sleeping up in that and that's where all the fire was. They must have had a candle up there for light that must have been knocked over.

Vetrini: When they started to throw down these vacant buildings in the city, they had an area down in Doremus Avenue-Wilson Avenue area where they were doing a lot of the dumping of these buildings. This dump pile from these buildings was at least twenty, twenty-five feet high and covered with some dirt. They had this dump fire. The companies were down there for one solid month. I don't know how many apparatus were burned out, two or three older rigs. They brought spare rigs down there to do the pumping. It got so that they wanted to take some of the weight off of the rigs pumping, so they took ten inch pipes from Weequahic Park and brought them down to the port, down to Doremus Avenue. These were used to take water from the river, bring it across Doremus Avenue, and into the dumps. There were two hook ups where pumpers were fed. Then they put one of the fireboats down at the bay to pump the pipe. That went on for maybe a week or so until one morning they went down to check the boat and the boat had sunk. That was the last time we had two fireboats.

*   *   *   *   *

Then another general alarm that we had was on Good Friday. By then we were working a forty-two hour week with four shifts. I hadn't been promoted yet. I had a fellow work for me, so I had to pay him back on Good Friday. This pier fire started. It was all wood pilings, creosote pilings. What happened was a small gasoline driven dredge with a crane on it was by the pier. For some reason the machine exploded and started the pier on fire at that point. Thirty-two Engine was first due. The first due captain lost his helmet when that crane fell. His helmet was under the crane. When we pulled in, the wind was blowing out toward the end of the pier. So we were chasing the fire out to the end of the pier with two and a half inch hoses.

Our fireboat, a Coast Guard boat, and a New York boat responded. Three engines took water from the bay. Ten Engine and Sixteen Engine left their hose wagons on the pier. Both were Ford hose wagons and they were exactly the same. All of the sudden the wind changed. Now the wind is pushing us back and it is getting so that the fire is coming up under us. We had to abandon lines and start moving back. They had to pull out the apparatus that were drafting. Captain Tangredi saw what he thought was his hose wagon. Now it's smoky. He jumps in the hose wagon and pulls it onto the land. Later we find out that he saved Sixteen Engine's and his own, Ten Engine's, burned.

Warren Petroleum

Vetrini: It was in the summer and we were out in front of quarters. A fellow stopped by and he said, "I just pulled the box on Ferry and St. Francis Streets. You have a fire down at the end of the street." Down at the end of the block was Cook and Dunn Paint. The bell was hitting. We got the operator. The captain told him that somebody reported it. They said, "We got it. We're sending an alarm in for Ferry and St. Francis." We got down to Ferry and St. Francis and these tanks were blowing like an atomic bomb mushroom. We thought it was the plant blowing up. We got down there. There was nothing. In the meantime, we were seeing another tank blow. Now it's on the air. There are companies moving down. They immediately called a second. That became a general alarm fire. There were companies from out of town that came in; which was a rarity at that time for companies to come into the city. Ironically, the Chief of the Department, the Deputy Chief, and Battalion Chief were at a meeting with the Warren Oil officials down by the docks talking about safety features. That's when the thing occurred.

When we got down there we couldn't go down Wilson Avenue to approach it at the onset. There were railroad cars on Doremus Avenue near where the Passaic Valley Sewage building was. The force of the tank blowing blew a coal car off the tracks maybe a half a mile from the explosion and bent it. A piece of the tank hit that car.

Engine Sixteen and Truck Eight were directed to go over the South Street ramp and come in on the Port Street side because companies were coming in from Doremus Avenue and Ferry Street. Ten Engine and the companies from that area were coming in over the highway. As we were coming over the ramp, I saw the dished end of one of those tanks, which were seventy feet long, ten feet high, and two inches thick fly from where it blew up. I estimate it went at least a half a mile out into the bay. It was flying like a Frisbee. Unbelievable. All we could do was protect the outer edges. International Printing Ink had a fire. We were at that one. Another plant on the other side caught, Four Truck, Twenty-seven Engine, and a few other companies got that. I don't know how many tanks blew. The farm had something like seventy tanks and more than thirty of them blew.

They had companies there through the night because there was one that was still burning. It was showing a flame at the vent. When we came back on duty the next day, we still had deluge sets keeping that tank cool until it burned out. It got so hot on some of the exposures that the tar on Doremus Avenue was burning. Whatever piece of tank blew to the street had the tar burning.

Kinnear: The propane fire in 1951 that everybody talks about, I was on vacation. Being a dedicated, caring fireman, I went to Six Engine to report. Six didn't even move on that fire. They stayed in quarters. The captain told me to go home. That was the biggest thing that happened in the early stages of my time on the job.

Vesey: We were going into work that night so they called us in. There was nothing we could do down there. Let it burn. I guess cover the other tanks, keep them cool.

Masters: I was on the engine when we had Warren Petroleum. I thought I was back in Europe with the devastation that those tanks flying created. I really mean it. Those tanks were, if I'm not mistaken, five feet in diameter. They were fifty feet long and half inch steel. They were flying off like rockets in Canaveral. One of them took off and landed right on a gas station, demolished the gas station. Another one took off, one in a million shot, came down on the ground, and broke a water main. So, we had to relay water from Newark Bay. I was at the dock with the Ahrens-Fox pumping water, relaying. We stayed there for three days.

When the alarm came in I was up in Irvington shopping with the wife. We were on our way home. I said, "Oh, my God look at that, must be in New York." I got close to my house and then we get a phone call. I had to report back to duty. Oh, I went right down, I lived on Farley Avenue then. They told me where to go and I went right there with my car. That's where I stayed. Then I had my brother-in-law come down and pick my car up. I went with Eleven Engine when I got there. I stayed there with the operator, helping him out.

That Ahrens-Fox shook so much, it sank right down in the mud to the hub caps. That's where it stayed. The only time it stopped was to check the oil and gas then started up again. They had to pull it out.

F. Grehl: I was a fireman at that thing. We were ordered to go down and report to the Coast Guard on the river. There are all these tanks in between the river and us. I was in Five Truck at the time. Twelve Engine was the one who was ordered to go down there. Jan Tausch was the captain. "Get on the back of the wagon. We'll sacrifice the wagon." But what about the men who were on back of the wagon? We were just getting ready to go and all of the sudden one of these tanks takes off like a rocket; shooting through the air with the fire coming out of the back. We all took off and ran. Fortunately, it never came near us. It hit a gas station down at Doremus Avenue and Wilson Avenue.

We finally re-grouped and we rode out. We're going through the middle of these tanks and suddenly one of them explodes. Willie Conover was the driver. I'll never forget him. They called him nervous Willie. He had to be nervous. He had to drive past one of these things. He lost everything off the apparatus but the men. We hung on. When we got to the other side by the river we had no equipment left.

We reported to the Coast Guard. They had a boat. We stretched hose line from there. We were stretching lines up. I think the guy who's in charge of the Coast Guard is a little kooky. We got a ladder and we went up over the fence, went down the other side. We went into the tanks and we're pouring this two and a half on this tank. I say to the guys on the Coast Guard, "Is this guy kooky or what? If this thing goes we're never going to get up over that fence and out of here." "He's a good man. We fought a lot of these fires. Don't worry about him." Well, all of the sudden he turns around to us. He says, "Okay, everybody out, up over that fence. Don't dilly-dally, move." We get up over the fence and down the other side. He says, "Okay, now start running for the river." We don't take twenty steps and that tank went boom.

We were running past a group of chiefs. Chief Burnett who was chief of the department, Chief Weeks and I think Chief Schoettly are there. One of the chiefs asks, "Where are you guys going?" when we started running. "The man ordered us out and we're going." He said, "We'll put you on charges for abandoning your position." "At least we'll be alive to be put on charges." The next thing you know "boom." When that thing blew I think old Weeks and those sixty year olds passed us.

McCormack: That was a large fire, explosion after explosion. The propane tanks were blowing up. You had the whole Newark Fire Department. They had a recall. I was off duty. I was sitting home having some lunch with my wife in the kitchen in the Roseville section. We had the radio on. All of the sudden they interrupted the radio broadcast and said because of this fire on Doremus Avenue all Newark firemen were ordered to report to their stations immediately, all off duty Newark firemen. I responded to the firehouse.

I saw those huge propane tanks blowing-up, some of them actually took off. Ripped off from their moorings and took off, went through the air like torpedoes. They flew hundreds of yards. One I remember draped over a gas station building it landed on, on Doremus Avenue and Wilson Avenue. The tank was over the roof of a gas station building. It was actually bent and twisted. It looked like one of those surrealistic paintings by Salvador Dali. The thing was rolled, laid, and twisted on top of the roof, hanging over the edges.

Deutch: Well, a fire that stands in my mind and I wasn't even on the job was Warren Petroleum. I could see those flames, balls shooting up in the air, from Vailsburg Park. I was playing ball with my future captain, Danny McCoy. He rushed right off the field and went back to work because he was on the fire department then. My dad was downtown and he walked down to the fire. Everybody was standing on a hill, which was just a mound from the Turnpike being built, watching that fire.

Redden: In Sixteen Engine fires down there were memorable because you had to stretch like twenty to forty lengths of hose sometimes. We had awful dump fires. You'd be down there for days, literally days.

Kinnear: I remember one fire, we were running on the second alarm from Ten Engine to one of the chemical places down on Doremus Avenue. The Deputy Chief, who was Tom O'Boyle at the time, had ordered us to stretch from Doremus Avenue. We stretched our ten lengths and we had to piece in another ten lengths to get to the fire. By the time we got there the fire was out.

*　*　*　*　*

Mostly, I remember going up on the hill though. Up to where Six Engine works and the big three story frames, tenements. A few other things along Frelinghuysen Avenue, rag storage places and things like that. But mostly they were up on the hill. The same as I was doing up at Six Engine.

F. Grehl: The fires really started when they started building the first project. The one across the street from Six Engine was really the first project they started building. I'm talking about the real high rises in the basic Central Ward. They had some others, up in Vailsburg and way down in the southern part of Newark down by Weequahic Park. They were the three or four story buildings, Bradley Court up in Vailsburg, too.

When they started the big high rises, naturally, they had to move all the people out. After they started moving the people out, the buildings were vacant before they got around to demolishing them. That's when we started with some real big, major fires. Because you'd have two or three buildings together and they'd have a stack of lumber where they knocked another one down. We always thought the builders set the fires. We never proved it nor did we have an Arson Squad at the time that was capable enough to prove it.

We thought these guys would set it on fire because it cost them money to knock the buildings down and take all this stuff away. These things would get going so good, the next thing you know they'd fall down. That's when we started on vacant buildings. There were a lot of them around. In the Fourth Battalion, we had three projects. So, we had lots of vacant buildings to work with in the Fourth.

That's when we got involved with master streams, because there was no sense in going in and trying to put the fires out. As things progressed and we got away from this particular situation, we got to areas where you had an isolated vacant building. You could stand outside and do what we called a surround and drown, but you might be there for two, three, four hours. We had talks about it. "Why don't we just get in and knock the thing down? It's nothing more than a two or three room job. Let's knock it down and get out of here so we're not here all night." We tried that to the point where they now have a vacant building that's been seriously weakened from the fire. They had a second fire. When do you go in? They started "x-ing" buildings that were too dangerous to go into. You have to flow with the trend. You have to make the changes as times change.

*　*　*　*　*

Memorable fires to me are ones where you had to think of a tremendous amount of things that were going on. What was left in the city? Hey, I'm all alone. I went as a Battalion Chief to a fire. I sent a second alarm and the acting chief at the time was Magnusson. They had two or three other fires going at the time. My second alarm was Twenty-eight, Thirty-two, and Twenty-six, my second alarm engine companies. In fact, Magnusson responded as Chief of the department before the second alarm companies got there. He says, "How are you making out?" I said, "I don't have anybody here yet and I have the third building going already. I've changed. I've moved Ten Truck's ladder pipe over and we're going to try and stop it there." He says, "You have to hold it there." I said, "I can't do anything until I get people." "The Director ordered you to hold it there." I said, "I can't hold it. What am I going to do?"

It got to the point where it started to get into the fourth building. At that time Twenty-six arrived and I put them into the building to try and stop it there. We just concentrated master streams there and just had to forget about the other buildings. But, something I was taught in school when I went on fire administration courses in New York. One of the things I was taught, if you need help, you call for it. If there's nobody left in the city that's not your problem, but you have to protect yourself in a court of law. Call for the help and if there's nothing there, that's not your problem. It's whoever is in charge. Now you go up another rank and on weekends you're the acting chief. Now you're the one who's in charge. Somebody could be doing it to you, too.

McCormack: I was a Captain at Two Truck. We had a cellar fire in a supermarket. We were told to put a hole in the floor and operate a cellar pipe through the hole. After we were fifty feet, seventy-five feet into the building, we squatted and then we crawled on our hands and knees dragging the hose with us. Just feeling the floor until we felt the floor was hot. That's where the fire was. We put a hole in the floor with an axe, put the hard cellar pipe through, and we're working there. There were three firemen and myself along with another company. They were right next to us in the smoke and they didn't have an officer with them. They only had an acting captain.

There was absolutely no visibility at all. It wasn't particularly hot, but the smoke was right down to the floor. You couldn't see anything. It was a helpless feeling. You couldn't see your hand in front of your face. But we had stretched a two and a half inch line in. That was our life line; our guideline to get back out again. That was weird.

All of the sudden, we heard this noise. It sounded like a freight train was coming through the building. It was awesome. Like a rolling, rumbling, rattling, continuous noise that didn't cease and it was building to a crescendo, getting bigger and bigger. We were all right where we were. Nothing seemed to be happening right in the spot we were, but we were in total darkness. We couldn't figure anything out. We didn't know where we were or what was going on. It was frightening. Everybody was like "What's the matter?"

I guess we were all thinking, "Is the building collapsing", but nothing was falling on our heads. The floor seemed okay where we were and our immediate vicinity seemed okay. Yet, this tremendous clattering, roaring, rolling noise is going on all around us. It's closing in on us. We can't even locate where the noise is coming from. It was loud. So everybody, I guess, was startled by it. What the heck, we didn't know what to do, whether to stay or run.

All of the sudden it dawned on me what it was. The floor was collapsing and these gondolas that held all the canned goods were pitching into the abyss. All these bottles and cans were rolling down. That's what the rumbling, rolling noises were. I couldn't see that, but I knew that's what it had to be. I said to my guys "We've got to get out of here. This place is going down."

I knew the guys from the other company that was in there didn't have an officer with them. I yelled for them and they didn't hear me. I yelled a couple of times. I had an idea they were over to my right. I marked where I was by the edge of something that was there and I just crawled over a bit to my right and I found them. They were in the next aisle. I told them "We have to get out of here." Somebody said to me in the smoke, "But Cap we can't go out, the Chief is going to yell at us." So needless to say we left. We simply followed the line back out and in a matter of a few seconds we were outside the building. I told people not to go in there.

Masterson: We had a fire on Emmet Street, that's only a couple of blocks from Ten Engine, so we were first due. We pulled up. This woman's out the window with her kids. They threw the ladder up. To my dismay, I hadn't even thought about it, the ladder didn't reach. But there's nobody coming and you could see the place was going. So, I went up. I got up to the top rung. I couldn't go any higher. I was in good enough physical shape I guess to balance myself up there. She hands the kids down. I grab them by the leg and give them down to Georgie Orlando. Two kids and I'm still waiting for the truck.

The truck was coming. Where the hell's the truck? I'm trying to tell her, "We'll get another ladder. We'll hold until the truck gets here." She wasn't staying up. She wasn't having any of that. She just sat her big ass out that window and came down and I just hung on. Are we both going to make it or what? So we were lucky. I just hugged the building with my weight. That's all you could do and I got down. I never even thought about it, never even thought about doing it. Never thought, you just did it. It had to be done.

* * * * *

Eddy Vesey and I came up to Five Truck together. I stuck with him. We were both riding the side of the apparatus. He showed me a few things I never knew could happen. We were on the roof opening up the roof. Eddy opens the scuttle and the stuffs coming out. Then he drops down to the third floor to check the third floor. I drop down with him. I said, "What the hell am I doing here?" because that stuff was rich. We search that third floor and we got down to the second floor. He was good. We had no masks. I wish I did.

Deutch: The fire that stands in my impression was the A & P fire. We had fires there twice, but the one time at night was a pretty bad fire, from the basement all the way up. It was the A & P Bakery which was on Petty Street and Frelinghuysen Avenue. That was a bad fire. I think that ended up going close to four alarms with all the extra apparatus.

I responded with Five Truck. We did a lot of truck work there, yes. Opening up. We were working the roof. Opened the roof up and put our portable pipe to work. We tried to get into the basement, but couldn't get in it was so hot down there. In fact we heard a lot of explosions, but that was from the columns. They were so hot the concrete was cracking off them. Eventually it went out, but it was a lot of fire. It was a night fire. That was one of my first fires.

Wall: You remember your close calls. We used to joke at the Squad that nine times out of ten when you got to a fire everybody's trying to get into the front door, so it leaves the back door wide open. We'd always try to take the back. We made some good rescues from the back. Danny McGee and I had gone around the back. We went up a ladder that was there and in across the third floor. I dropped right through the floor. It was burned out. The only reason I didn't go through was McGee literally tackled me and held me until I could get my hands on the beams. Then he pulled me out. That part you remember and you remember the value of having a good partner.

McGee: Very early in the job, I was in Eleven Truck. We had a fire on Seventh Street. The normal procedure was to bring a twenty-four foot ladder in with you into the alleyway. It was a very heavy smoke condition. In that area alleyways were literally arms' length from the next building. We raised this ladder because there was a fellow sitting in the third floor window and he was on his way out. That's how much heavy smoke was coming out of the windows. The ladder was short. We didn't have time to go back and get another ladder. Chief Schaeffer said, "Put that ladder on your shoulders." Two big firemen from Eleven Truck put the ladder on their shoulders. I climbed up the ladder because I was the smallest, skinniest guy.

We brought the man down the ladder. That man definitely would have died. That was very impressive to me because it was one of the earliest fires that I went to. What I'm saying is impressive is not so much for my part because it's probably the easiest part. The two guys backed themselves up against the other building, which was close enough to hold them, and raised the ladder. I climbed up, literally climbed up one of the guys, climbed up the ladder, and brought the man down. What impressed me the most was the Chief had the presence of mind to realize that we didn't have time to back out and get another ladder. Had we raised that ladder it would have been maybe eight or ten feet lower than where the man was. He would have never gone on that ladder and we might have even been hurt. In those days there wasn't this big commendation thing. I think we got a commendation, but it was not put to the burn center or anything. In fact, our Chiefs used to say, "That's what you get paid for."

Stoffers: There was a feud between Chief Donlon and Chief Drew. This is my understanding of how the feud started. Hilliard was the Chief Engineer temporarily, Joe Drew was the First Deputy, and Donlon was the Fourth Battalion Chief. They were on the third tour. Everything was going along fine. In those days, the Deputy would go down to see the Chief his first day in to see what was going on. So, Drew goes down to see Hilliard. Hilliard says to him, "Oh, hello Joe. How's Donlon? Still running your Deputy Division?" Drew comes back to the firehouse. He's upstairs in his room. Donlon comes in. "Where's the Chief?" "Upstairs." He goes upstairs and walks in the room. "Hi, Chief, how are you?" Sits on the bed. Drew says, "Get off that bed." And that's when the thing started.

We get a fire one day. It's about three o'clock in the afternoon. Up near Belmont and Mercer and nothing was showing. The box was Springfield and Belmont so everybody went to the box. We had a spare apparatus. We're coming down Belmont Avenue and all of the sudden these people start waving. "What's the matter?" "There's a fire up here." "Oh, okay." We can't see anything, but we call, "We may have something here." We go up. When we get to the top floor, it's coming out of the kitchen, right across the hallway. "You better get a line up here." Drew was coming down from Avon Avenue. Donlon calls in a three hundred. We said, "We may have something here Chief." He comes back and now it's Five Truck and Twelve Engine. "What do you have?" "We have a job on the top floor." We stretch in the hose, went to work like crazy. Oh, we busted our ass. We hear Drew on the radio calling, "What do you have down there, Chief?" "Oh, nothing. We have a three oh five here. We're going to take care of it."

McGrory: My first good job, we had a three-story frame on West Runyon down near Bergen Street. A lot of us had rubber turn out coats, rubber boots, and the leather helmets. I'm riding on the back with Willie Quirk and we had our coats draped over the back handrail. It's blowing out the third floor windows of a three-story frame. It's a hot summer day, during the day. I did everything Willie did. He jumped off, threw his coat on the ground. I threw my coat on the ground. He grabbed a two and a half. I grabbed a two and a half. We start pulling the two and a half off.

Now we're going to go upstairs. Captain Brock is yelling. We don't stand on the outside. We take this two and a half to the third floor without masks. I think I got my coat on. We have to wait for water. We're in the staircase and the whole cockloft's going. The third floor is going. It's a six family duplex, three-story frame. We got on the left side. We're going up, can't get up to the third floor landing. We have to wait. We have fire all over. We hit it and it just banks down on us. He yells for me, "Go get a mask!" I run all the way down to the corner. Grab two masks. Run all the way back. Give him a mask.

By that time Danny McCoy is on a two and a half inch line. Willie yells to me, "Put your mask on kid!" I'm panting, but I put my mask on. I get up and Danny McCoy and I go in with that. They're lightening up. Danny yells to me, "Tell them to lighten up!" The truck men are coming up the stairs. "Lighten up!" "Get the hell out of here." So, we go in. The truck gets the roof, but I'm telling you it's hot. My eyes are crossing. I'm bow legged. I'm exhausted because of the excitement, running, and heat.

We get in. We work our way into the front room. By that time somebody else comes up behind us and they go into the rear. Danny McCoy gets it pretty well knocked down then he gives the line to me. "Hey, kid. Hold this line up in the air." He walks over to wave out the front window.

Now he doesn't know that I can't control it too well. I almost knocked him out the front window. By that time, I'm just staggering around.

The Deputy asked, "What's the matter with you, kid?" Then he told me, "Go sit over there." I go into another apartment and sit in a big, overstuffed chair. I'm sitting there. My tongue is hanging out. I'm finished. I can't move. Now, they all have to come up, "What's the matter with you." I can't even talk. I'm saying to myself, "What the hell did I take this job for? This is crazy."

Denvir: Five Truck had broken down and we got the extra call. We went all the way over to their area. They said there were five kids in the building. We went up. They had knocked the fire down. There was still a lot of smoke. We went up on the fire escape. Bill Olvaney, Captain Marron from Twenty, and Rocco Piegaro were on the fire escape.

I went in the window first and then Stanley Kossup came in behind me. I said, "You go to the right and I'll go to the left." It was a small room. I found a doorway and went into the room. I felt a leg. "Stan, I've got one. I've got a kid here." So, I passed it to him and he handed him out the window. I went back and I found another one and handed it to him. Found another one and handed it to him. Now they're going out the window. When I found the little baby I handed it to him. There was nobody else there so he went out the fire escape and passed it down. I went and found the other one. They were twins. I passed them out and that's where that picture was taken. He went out on the fire escape and gave it mouth to mouth and brought it around. I went looking to see if there were any more kids. But there were none. You'd never forget that. We were only on the job about a year when that happened. That's a good memory. They all made it.

* * * * *

New Year's Eve 1960, we had about four multiple alarm fires that night. The first one was on Jones Street. That went to a deuce. We were on the roof on Jones Street. They said they had a fire over on Seventh Street. That went to four alarms. We could see the smoke. When we finished at Jones Street, we went back to quarters and were cleaning up. A guy from Thirty-two Engine was pumping on Sixth Street and Seventh Avenue. He said, "I think you have a fire down on Sixth Street." That was a big factory that went up. At the same time they had a fire on Broadway and Verona. At that time, that was Newark's busiest night, New Year's Eve 1960. That was my first year on the job.

It's funny why I remember that. Sam Magano and I were on the roof. We were opening up and Sam was standing right next to me. The next thing Sam was gone. It collapsed on him, collapsed underneath him. But most of the fire was out. So we jumped down the ladder. He was laughing. That's why that always stuck in my mind, seeing Sam disappear.

*   *   *   *   *

I don't recall where the fire was, but there was a child trapped in the building. The fire was on the first floor. They didn't know where the kid was. We came in, went around the back. Eddie Jankowski went in the second floor. Dick Kelly and I went to the third floor looking. I went into a room and the door closed behind me. I went around the room and I was having a hard time finding the door. We had the canister mask on, but the breathing wasn't too good. It was a little warm, but I was starting to panic. Am I going to find my way out of this room? I finally get out of the room. "Now where's the door to get out of the building?" I only did one room. Then I heard a door. I said, "Who's that?" He says, "It's Jankowski." I grabbed hold of him. "Boy, am I glad to see you." He said, "They found the kid downstairs." Skippy Linhoff had grabbed the kid in one of the bedrooms on the first floor. I followed Jankowski down the stairs. That I've never forgotten.

Freda: I was trying to impress my captain at one of the first fires I ever had. Show how brave I was. It was a job on Bloomfield Avenue in an interior decorator place. I was there no more than two minutes. I ran in the front door. A beam came down, hit me on the head, and knocked me the hell out. I'd say five minutes after the fire started I was outside, knocked out. Doctor Ciccone, who was the fire surgeon then, examined me and said, "You have a little concussion, go home." And I remember within an hour of me dropping my wife off at her mother's house, I was back at her mother's house telling this harrowing story of how I was almost killed at this fire. I remember Doctor Ciccone telling me, "If you get nauseous call me up because it could mean something else." I threw up all night and I never told him. I said to hell with it because I wanted to go to work the next night.

* * * * *

While I was at Twelve Engine, we had a fire in an A and P. We were inside this store after pouring tons and tons of water into the cockloft. The roof came down. There were several of us trapped. It's probably the only time in my career that I thought I was going to be killed. Surprising enough, I wasn't afraid. I felt the roof coming down. It was pressing on me. I said, "This is it." By instincts I took off like a rabbit. That's the only way to describe it. I crawled in between the checkout counter with the great majority of the stuff falling across the checkout counter. I was still buried, but the majority of the weight was across the checkout counters. Gerry Knight was a few feet away. He was totally buried along with several more people.

What was I thinking of while I was lying in there trapped? It dawned on me that I wasn't killed. There was no fear then. I really didn't have one second of fear while trapped. I just accepted it as the inevitable. I remember hearing the chief say outside the building, "Captains, count your men. Give me a count of your men." And that struck me as being humorous because I figured, "Now, who the hell is going to count me? I'm the captain and I'm in here."

Frankie Calvitti jumped into a shopping cart, flew across the floor, and went right out the front window. You have to give him credit. It was a good move. Then when they finally dug us out, they couldn't find Gerry Knight. I remember this as if it was yesterday. They heard Gerry Knight yelling, "Get off my head." I looked over and I saw Eddie Chrystal, who was a Deputy Chief, standing on Gerry Knight's head because I knew where Gerry Knight was. Nobody else knew. I remember telling Eddie Chrystal to please get off Gerry Knight's head. You're standing on the man's head. They dug him out. He wasn't seriously injured. He was out of service for a few months, but he wasn't hurt. We were all lucky that we weren't killed.

But the fear set in later on. It took me several months to gain my confidence back to go into a fire building. I was very, very cautious at even the mundane fires after that. But then gradually as the months past I went back to my old reckless self. And that's what happens until you become experienced. That's how you get hurt sometimes. I got back into the competition and it became more important than my own safety.

I don't know if it was a truss roof. In fact, at that time I probably didn't even know what the hell a truss roof was. We didn't have that type of training. I wouldn't have known one if you pointed it out to me. I know they had several deck guns and ladder pipes pouring onto the roof, pouring tons of water into the cockloft. It was the water really that sent the whole building down on us. And it really rolled down, slowly. It wasn't a fast action. I saw it coming. It was almost like slow motion. The front went and it gradually went inch by inch. It came down real slow.

I remember it pushing and I remember the pressure on my back. I remember being forced to the floor. It sounds scary now, but I don't know why. I wasn't scared. I thought I was going to be killed. I accepted the fact. I thought it was inevitable. I knew I couldn't do a damned thing about it. I didn't think of anything. You hear people say, "My family." Nothing. I just said, "This is it." But in that split second I saw the checkout counter and that's where I headed by instinct. That's probably what saved me from being hurt severely.

Charpertier: During one snow storm there was an oil spill fire on Fairmount Avenue, which in normal times would have been knocked down in five or ten minutes. It wound up with three buildings going. You couldn't get in Fairmount Avenue from Sixteenth Avenue because the snow was piled two stories high. We had to hump lines up over the snow bank and then drag it half way into the middle of the block to even get a water supply. It was rough.

Dunn: The fire that comes to my mind was in 1960 on Good Friday. I was at Twenty Engine. We had what I call my first major fire, a trestle fire in the East Ward. It was a Central Railroad trestle. That turned out to be a four-alarm fire. Because of the ember problem and a heavy, windy condition, that fire wound up burning about thirty buildings. Most of them were roof fires. The fire was spreading over several blocks and you just couldn't keep up with it. It just stripped the Newark Fire Department out of its resources because alarms were coming in from maybe a quarter of a mile area for roof fires. You had nobody to send so every now and then the roof fire turned into a big fire and you had another house burning three or four blocks away from where you were operating. I always remember that trestle. Today it's a telephone repair yard. That fire took care of the trestle problem.

Smith: The first multiple I ever went to was a four alarm fire on Stratford place. That was a whole row of connected apartment buildings that burned. Then there was a five alarm fire down on Market. Then you had the five alarm fire down in the dumps, a tire fire. There were a lot of them. Multiples not because of a lack of manpower, it was simply because the volume of fire was so large. Then there was the fire down off South Street where there was a loss of life because they had a thirty gallon drum of kerosene on the back porch of each floor. They used to use the kerosene heaters. They used to go out and fill them. The porch became soaked with kerosene.

I don't know if they were within the fire code. It had been in existence for so long. I remember as a kid, we had it out in the back yard because we had kerosene heaters in the house. But the up keep of them was done by my father and we were forbidden to go near them, even my mother. We never had a fire because they were cleaned, trimmed and my father inspected them to see whether there were leaks or not.

Carragher: I remember in Nine Engine when I first came on the job on West Street. I think it was like twenty vacant buildings that burned. It was a row and the whole row burned. Up above on Charlton Street, we had three or four or five other buildings burning up the street. That's why Nine Engine was due on Charlton Street on the first alarm because of the fire on West Street. It was a cover with a couple of big fires going at the same time.

*   *   *   *   *

We had the rug factory on Third and McCarter Highway. At the time it was a two million dollar loss, which you figure in 1960, two million dollars is a big loss. That was a big building and a two alarm fire. We relieved at that. I guess I had Art Metals, which is on Passaic Street. That was a three-alarm fire.

*   *   *   *   *

When I was a fireman coming down to Twenty Engine, we had the tire fire on Avenue P, Wilson and Avenue P, Verone's dumps. We were down there quite a while. That was a major fire, a three alarm fire. We were down there a couple of times. One time going down there, they put us back in service and we caught another fire over off of Elizabeth Avenue. I think we had three three-story frame buildings burning there. The only thing that really saved that fire is Five Truck. Five Truck carried lengths of inch and a half hose. They hooked up to a hydrant near the front of the building. They went to work with the inch and a half and saved the fire from spreading down the street. They did a good job there. Five Truck did it just off the hydrant.

*   *   *   *   *

Another one we had when I was at Six Engine on South Orange Avenue one night, a three-alarm fire again. We pulled up. Freddy Charpentier was driving. No hydrants and I saw a high-pressure hydrant. Well, up until this time you never hooked up to a high-pressure hydrant with a pumper. That was the standing rule on the fire department. I said, "Freddy hook up to that high-pressure." "What do you mean hook up? You can't do it. It's against the rules." Well, we fed two or three deck pipes from that high-pressure hydrant and had our own. That really showed. We had this Ward. That Ward could pump. It was a piece of junk, but it could pump. It did the number. We had a death at that fire. We had a guy buried in the building somewhere, never got him out.

* * * * *

I also remember another one as a captain in Seven Engine going at Sixteenth Avenue and Twelfth Street, on the corner was a three story frame. I went up on the second alarm with Seven. We were called to take a line in the back way. We had eight deaths in that fire. I think myself, Harry Uhde, John Hughes, and Ray McGee found about four of the bodies crawling across the floor on the second floor. That was on the twenty-third of December, 1965.

* * * * *

When I was the Fourth Battalion Chief, I had so many fires. When I think of all the apartment houses we had over on Johnson Avenue, Hillside Avenue, Hillside Place, Hillside Terrace, and Belmont Avenue. It was nothing to see four or five buildings burning at one time. When I say four or five buildings, I probably had at least a hundred fires with four or five buildings burning in my career.

Harris: The first big fire I ever had was right across the street from Twenty Engine. We had a four-alarm fire. There was a factory right next door to a church, right directly across. Captain Schoemer and myself and somebody else, we took a line to the top of the church roof. Thick ice on the roof and every time I take a step, I'm sliding back. Schoemer's reaching out. "Come on kid, you can make it. You're going to have to do this the rest of your career." And he's hollering. What is wrong with this man? We better get the hell off of here.

So, we get up there and we get to the chimney and we kind of brace ourselves, locking our arms around the chimney. Trying to control this line and shoot it into the top of the building next door. Then finally somebody said, "Off the roof." We get to the edge of the roof. Somebody took our ladder. We don't have a ladder. Schoemer starts calling. I don't know who it was. Somebody brought our ladder back over and put it back. But we had no ladder to get down. Not long after we had gotten down, part of the church roof and the roof of the fire building went. The church roof went only because this building collapsed on to it.

As they were giving us a break, I went across the street to Twenty Engine, freezing. I mean you couldn't even take my coat off. It was frozen solid. I said to myself then, "This ain't no God damn job for me. I'm quitting. That's it. I'm not going to do this."

They had put us to work as an engine company fighting the fire at first. Now once the fire got knocked down, we had to go into the church and start covering the pews and the altar. When we got back to the firehouse, I'm sitting down. We're drinking the coffee and I'm saying to myself, "I quit. I quit. I'm not doing this. I didn't know you had to be up two stories on an icy roof. You're going to slide back down. This doesn't make any damn sense to me." That was my first big job.

Haran: One of my first fires within my first couple of weeks on the job was probably one of my worst fires ever. It was on Broad and Camp Streets, down by Pennington there just on the other side of 1060 Broad Street which was the old draft board. I'll never forget. We used to pull out of Salvage. We'd come up Lafayette Street and make our left onto Broad Street. Ten Engine, One Engine, and One Truck were the first two engines and truck on it. We turned the corner and the sky was lit up. We pulled in. I saw one of the best rescues I've ever seen on the Newark Fire Department that never got mentioned.

I worked with a fellow by the name of John Miele. His name was Luciano Miele. He was an older fellow, good shape. I tell this story quite often when guys start talking about rescues because I've seen one of the greatest rescues on the Newark Fire Department and the guy never even got a mention.

What had happened was we pulled around coming off of Lafayette Street onto Broad Street. The sky was lit up. We could see it down on our left hand side. So we pulled down there and sure enough there was this three story duplex, three story six family house that they were using for senior citizen housing. There were people in there with wheel chairs, sickly, elderly. There was a fellow in One Truck at the time by the name of Artie Farrow. He went to go into the front door. Somebody jumped off the third floor. As he got to the top of the stairs, they landed on top of him and broke both his legs. That was just one of the things that developed down at this fire. That same fire, we're on Salvage Corps, so we had two ladders. We had a sixteen foot roof ladder and a twenty-four foot two piece extension ladder. We didn't take them off. The building was a three story, six family home with a one story garage right next door to it.

John Miele went over to one of the trucks there, pulled a sixteen foot roof ladder off the truck. Threw it up to the one story garage, went up, pulled the ladder up onto the one story garage because there was a guy hanging out the third floor window against the side of the building who wasn't going to be hanging there in another minute. He pulled the ladder up behind him and he pinned the guy to the building and he held him there until the truck could come in with other ladders and take the guy off the side of the building. He pinned him there between the two rails of the ladder. To me that was one of the best rescues I ever saw. Quick thinking, to pull a ladder off a truck, up to the garage, pull the ladder up on top of the garage, run across the garage roof, and pin the guy against the building until they were able to take him down and never get an honorable mention.

Highsmith: Well, my first memorable fire was my first big fire. I was on the book and somebody started knocking at the door and the bells started hitting at the same time. I lifted up the overhead door and the guy said, "There's a fire down the street." So, I looked down Frelinghuysen Avenue going north and I saw a fire rolling out in the street, actually rolling in big balls out in the street. I hit the bell. Everybody comes downstairs. We jump on the engine and we go down to the fire. The fire is still rolling down the street. We put up a ladder to the roof because it took One Truck a while to get there and Five Truck a while and Ten Truck a while to get over. So, we're going to see what we can do on the roof. Try and ventilate or something, get some water in there. Mistake for me.

I get up on the roof. I lose my partner. I'm surrounded by nothing but smoke, my first big fire. I said, "Lord if I ever get off this roof. I'm quitting this job." So, I thought about what little training I had. I got down on my hands and my knees and I crawled and I groped and I groped until I found the ledge of the roof. Then from the ledge of the roof, I groped all the way around until I found the ladder. I said, "No Lord, you trained me enough to keep me on this job." Then I got down. That was one of the most horrifying events then because I was brand new on the job. Then Freddy grabbed me and he cussed me out for getting lost up on the roof. I'm not supposed to be up there without anybody. Make sure somebody's with me and I started learning.

*   *   *   *   *

We had a fire on Milford Avenue. As we pulled in there we started fighting the fire and Captain Finucan looked at me. He said, "Did you ever see a dead body before?" I said, "No." And he took me into a room. He said, "Look this is not the last one you're going to see, but look at it because this is what you're going to be seeing throughout your career." I looked at it. That was the first body I saw.

*   *   *   *   *

We fought Ricciardi's Paint up on Belmont Avenue. That's when I got more respect for Freddy Scalera. We pulled up there on about the fourth alarm and everybody was down fighting the fire. We stopped in front of Twelve Engine on Belmont Avenue. They had a hydrant in front of the firehouse and a hydrant across the street. Both of them had very little pressure. Freddy hooked up to both of the hydrants and we stretched it a long block with that big three inch. Freddy gave us all the water we wanted by hooking up to two hydrants. He could get water. Wherever there was water, he could get water. Wherever there was an outlet, he could give you water. That's one thing he taught me.

When I was an engine driver, always when the wagon is ready, you must be ready with the water. I always prided myself, when I drove the engine and hooked up, by the time unit two called to unit one, which was me in the engine, he said, "Gerry, give us water." First thing I said was, "You've got it." All I had to do was pull it out. The teaching that I got from the guys I worked with.

Garrity: My first fire was a three story frame over on New and Arlene which is where they built Rutgers. I remember because after we had the fire knocked down, my captain came over and says, "Come here kid, I want to show you something." So he brings me over to the corner, it's all dark, and he shines a flashlight on this guy. He was burned in the corner. It's my first job, my very first job I had. It turned out he was murdered and that's what the fire was all about. I guess I was supposed to have some kind of sick reaction. Obviously, he's dead. I worked for a funeral director once in a while, so dead bodies didn't bother me too much.

My captain's instructions to me the first night I went to work were, "I want you to grab the back of my mask strap and don't let go until I tell you. And just follow me wherever I take you." Those were his only instructions to me. He showed me where my bed was. He gave me a locker and then I didn't see him the rest of the night. Those were his instructions. The fire was the second night. I think we had one run to the projects or two runs to the projects and nothing after that. Of course, I couldn't sleep all night lying in bed waiting for the bells to ring. The next night we had the fire on New and Arlene.

*   *   *   *   *

We had a fire one afternoon on Mount Pleasant Avenue off Clay Street. About ten o'clock in the morning we went over to this pharmaceutical factory. The alarm was going off. We went through the building and found no fire. We took up. Malfunction of the alarm system. We get back to the firehouse. About an hour later, we get the box again. We get back over there; the whole top floor was going, from one end to the other. It was coming out the windows.

I got up on the roof. We were shorthanded, so I was working alone on the roof. I hear this voice behind me say, "What do you have here kid?" And I say, "What the do you think we have? We have a fire." It was Chief McLaughlin. I immediately expected to get kicked in the ass or something. He turns to his driver and he says, "Stevie, you better send a second alarm. It looks like it's going real good." And he just walked away. He never said a word to me after that. I mean he never mentioned it again. Never said, "Who do you think you're talking to?"

That was not Chief McLaughlin if you knew him. He had a comeback for everybody. No matter who you were. He never bothered me. He never picked on me. Everybody said he would pick on you. He did come in one time and ask me what a manger adapter was. He said, "Get me your manger adapter." and I went over and I got it. He used to bust the whole company's balls, but he didn't individually pick on me where he did do that to a lot of young guys. He would come into the firehouse and pick on you. He was just a ball buster.

We went to a fire. We got on the top floor, had this place full of smoke, so we broke all the windows on the top floor. It turned out to be a coat in the closet. He came back and he said, "You guys screwed up a little bit. If I need a truck company, you're gonna be it." And he special called us for about a week for different things. He'd have a special drill for us and stuff like that

*   *   *   *   *

Another job we had was on Passaic Street, one of those factories up there. It wasn't a big one, but it was long. It was like maybe a one story where the trucks would pull in and it was a two story brick alongside it. They had this big open overhead rolling door between the two buildings. We got there. There's this heavy fire condition in the two story section, but you could walk into where the truck loading dock was. We walked into the truck loading dock and Nine Engine had set up a two and a half. From this whole loading dock door there's a wall of fire.

It was me and Vito Finetti. We walked up to the door. There was this loud explosion and flames came shooting out of this doorway. It shot out about ten feet and got sucked back in again. He started to run. Nine Engine shut their line down as we ran out. There was now water on the floor and this little ramp going up to the sidewalk had oil on it. Our feet are moving and we're tripping over one another. Now we start to laugh because we're falling all over the place. Another one lets go. Now everyone thinks this whole place was coming down. We were crawling out of the place. You never saw anything like it in your life. It was assholes and elbows getting out of this place. Turns out that they had some tow motors in there with propane on them and they had storage for propane. They were blowing up.

After we get out of the building, Vito said to me, "Let's go over and see what we can do, see what's going on." So we went over to a window which was just over our eyes. He put his hands on the window sill and pulled his eyes and nose up and another one let go. For the rest of the night he wouldn't go near the building until the fire was out. Wouldn't go near it. I pissed in my pants laughing at him.

The Military Park Hotel

Dunn: When I was a newly appointed captain to Twelve Engine we had the Military Park Hotel fire. I believe it occurred on Christmas Eve. The alarm came in around one o'clock in the afternoon. Captain Florio in One Engine came over the radio with the message that he had fire coming out the front door of the Military Park Hotel. Certainly, that picks up everybody's interest because it's something you just don't expect to hear. You could hear the excitement in his voice. Numerous rescue problems existed. It was communicated over the radio and within the first two or three minutes they went to a three-alarm assignment with extra trucks being called.

We were sitting in Twelve Engine at the time still not assigned to the fire. Probably within ten minutes a fourth alarm was sounded with another additional special call, which sent Five Truck and us to the Military Park.

You have to remember this was all prior to losing Two Truck and Three Truck.

Upon arrival, you can imagine the commotion and confusion that was there with that kind of an assignment that quickly. People were Christmas shopping in downtown Newark. There were numerous large Christmas parties in a major hotel involved in heavy fire. Nobody had accountability for anything. Twelve Engine and Five Truck weaseled their way into the back of the hotel. We found a rear fire staircase. Captain McCoy and I started ascending the staircase. Probably around the fourth or fifth floor of this hotel, which is twelve stories high, we start to encounter heavy smoke. As we proceeded up the staircase we started running into people from Douglas Construction Company. They were at a Christmas party there. These people were overcome. They were in a panic state in heavy smoke conditions. Between Twelve Engine and Five Truck, we probably pulled out of that back staircase anywhere from ten to fifteen people. Unfortunately, one or two of them succumbed to the gases.

I think of the dramatic effect of it being a Christmas Eve fire. Certainly, it had a lot of ramifications. I always remembered the look of these people on the staircase, where in an evacuation you're supposed to do it by size and age and in an orderly manner. But when you run into a group of people of this number in a panicked state, you just grab the first one you can and try to bring them down. You can't go up and down a flight of stairs too often. I found that out very quickly.

What we found out as we proceeded through this rescue operation was there was a door missing from the fire floor of the hotel. That's why the smoke went into the fire tower. The fire tower was designed so that you can come from any floor out into the fire tower. As these people entered the fire tower and tried to proceed down, they were going against the heat and smoke that came in, so they went up, which was a normal reaction. The only problem is when they got to the top floor, there's a skylight in that stair tower that's probably about sixteen foot high. Nobody could reach it. The doors only opened from the floor out onto the stairwell. There was no way for the people to get out. They were afraid to go down. The smoke got them.

If we had it all to do over again, we probably should have gone above and let all the people in there, then tried to break the skylight out with our hooks or something like that. But not realizing what was going on at the time, we did what we thought was a very orderly evacuation of a large number of people.

The surprise was the fact that firefighting was going on in the hotel. Firefighting personnel were all through the hotel trying to search rooms. And yet we came in there very late in the fire and discovered a very large number of people. A third of them were overcome. As I said, one or two of them succumbed to the smoke, and yet we couldn't get the resources to quickly evacuate the stair tower because we couldn't communicate what we found. We weren't sure what we found. When I found the guy, I didn't know there were fifteen guys above him in this smoke. It always had a lasting impression on how lucky those people were to be alive today. It could have been a major fire loss in the city. I think five people died in the hotel throughout different areas, but fortunately only one in that back tower.

The ironic part was they did what they were supposed to do. They were led to the rear fire staircase that should have led them right out into a parking lot. But because over the years, somebody took a fire door off, these people wound up in a death trap situation. If it wasn't for Five Truck and Twelve Engine trying to find a sneaky way into the hotel, no one would have discovered these people were trapped there. I don't think anybody would have ever opened the doors to that stairway until long into this fire. Because you couldn't get above the lobby fire quickly and find this in a rear entrance of a major hotel that's probably 200 by 200. So these people probably would have succumbed.

I felt when I came home from that fire, that it was one of the premier operations working with Five Truck and Twelve Engine. Another thing Five Truck did was raise their forty-five ladder up to the roof after the rescue to find if there were any more people up there. It's not easy to do that after you did the search and rescue. I look back at that fire from a firefighting point of view with some fine memories of doing an excellent job and feeling good about it. It also solidified my crew's trust in me as their captain.

A Christmas tree was your basic fire and some content in the lobby. The fire never did communicate up the staircase because there was nothing to burn in the staircases. That was a real Christmas tree of probably twenty, twenty-five, thirty feet tall with Christmas lights on it. There was a short in the lights and the tree flashed because it was in the hotel probably from the fifteenth on in the heated conditions. There was no stopping that fire. The fire was confined to that first floor area.

But the products of combustion certainly did get up there and got trapped up there. Had the fire door been in place, those people would have been able to walk down and out the back exit of that fire and into the parking lot. They never did find out how long that door had been removed. That was a contributing factor to the death of one or two people and the trapping of fifteen people in that rear staircase.

The other thing that fire did was from then on the use of live Christmas trees in public buildings has been frowned upon. That became part of the Bureau of Fire Safety laws in New Jersey.

Miller: I was the acting captain at Two Truck when we got the Military Park Hotel fire. I remember we fully extended the aerial ladder up to the front of the building. We were the first truck company there. We got some people out of the window. At that time they had no water. While the aerial was going up, I went into the lobby. It was completely ablaze. You couldn't go in there without a mask. There were some people in there at the time. The hotel telephone operator was still in there. I think she died notifying people. She was burned very badly.

It was roaring. We had to wait for the other companies to get water. The second alarm was sounded. That was a very tragic fire. Most of our job was going up the back stairways in the dark where the people had tried to get up to the roof. They were all on the top floor. They couldn't get out to the roof. So we had to go up there and carry them down on our backs or help them down. They were in a dazed condition.

Garrity: The Military Park Hotel fire was the first day I drove, December 24, 1964. We pulled up in front of that building. Flames blew out the top of the mezzanine level and there were people hanging out the window on the sixth floor. We put the ladder up. We got three people out of the window and came back down. As we were going back in the front door, the chandelier in the center crashed to the floor. Luckily they had gotten beyond that point. But that fire was out in no time and we had I think eleven people dead in there. It was an unreal fire. It just burned that whole first floor and filled the whole place with smoke. They had the doors all propped up. The people upstairs and the telephone operators, all died of smoke inhalation. Found a woman in the bathroom, on the floor. Not a mark on her. Not even soot. She was dead from smoke.

That is my most memorable fire of all the fires I fought. It scared the living daylights out of me. It really did. It wasn't the most spectacular fire once it got knocked down, but that's the first time I had multiple deaths at a fire. First time I ever made a high level rescue. Things like that. One of the sidebars to that is my sister was shopping in Haynes when that happened. She saw all the fire engines and the smoke. She came across the park to watch what was going on. I saw her. We had taken the people out of the window. I don't know whether she saw that or not. I was doing something at the side of the truck. Probably not putting on a mask, but doing something. She waved to me and I waved back. Then I just went inside. She called my mother and said, "I saw him go in the building and I never saw him come out again." Of course, she was only there about a half an hour. But my mother was a basket case for quite a while.

Chapter Three: The Unusual

Fredette: Down around Baldwin Street in the '40s and the '50s, there were a lot of stables there. You used to be able to rent a horse and a wagon for three dollars a day. A guy would go out peddling, either a rag man or get vegetables and peddle them. There had to be between twenty and twenty-five horses down there. They had a lot of manure pits. The straw in the manure would cause a spontaneous ignition. You could stay there for days. All we did was take the nozzle off the two and a half, stick the open butt down, turn on a hydrant, and just flood it out. First thing you knew, all the horseshit would come floating out of the top, but that is the only way you can put out a manure pit.

Vetrini: The fat and tallow places. They got all the fats and bones from the butchers. They took it down there and they cooked it. They screened it and they used that for soaps and whatever else. We used to get that quite often because their housekeeping was very bad. If one of their machines overheated, then all that grease would take off. No such thing as housekeeping, none what so ever. It was nice fun at 3 o'clock in the morning. You would walk in there and see a horse's head sticking out of a bucket or something, with his eyes peering at you.

Masters: We had this one fire, a bedroom fire. So naturally what do you do with the mattress? Heave it out into the yard. Well, I tell you, a woman comes in. "*Materasso*, where's the *materasso*?" I talk Italian, so I said, "It's in the yard." Okay. She goes out in the yard, gets on her knees, puts her arm in the mattress; pulls out a wad of money. Another time, we're overhauling in the kitchen. We pulled the refrigerator away from the wall. "Hey, look what's in here." Five, ten dollar bills all taped to the refrigerator. Another time we had a fire in a cop's house. We knew the cop. He lived on Thirteenth Avenue and Ninth Street; had a fire in the second floor apartment. We're overhauling. Pull out the draw, money. So I say, (whispers) "Hey Cap, hey DePaul, look." "Oh my God, sit on that." So, the cop's outside. He goes, (whispers) "Come on up." Came up. "Take that out." Got a big plastic bag, took the whole drawer out. It was all money. I don't know how much. Puts it in, went out. Oh, he saved the money. I think he was Scotch and he saved money.

Another time about two-thirty in the morning, you don't sleep because the two taverns are letting out, one on Central Avenue and Ninth Street and the one down in the middle of the block. There's an argument going in front of the firehouse and we're all up watching this argument and hollering. A man and a woman are fighting and the woman is fighting just like a man. She rips the guy's shirt right off his back and that's when it all started. They're duking it out so, one of our colored firemen said to the other colored boy, Larry Polite, "I'm going out to stop them." So, Larry said, "Mind your own business." He had been a prison guard. He said, "Mind your own business." "Oh, I can't let them. Look what he's doing to that woman." "Yeah, but look what the woman's doing to the guy." So, he goes out and the both of them turn on the colored fireman, beating him up. So, he comes into the firehouse, putting his hands to his head. Larry says, "Didn't I tell you to mind your own business. You don't interfere with other people's arguments or fights."

*   *   *   *   *

We went to the City Hospital to get instructions on how to deliver babies. So, we went for a whole week. They supplied us with sterile clean sheets in plastic bags. The engine had them and the truck had them. A women came in, "I'm going to have a baby. My water busted." I said,

"Let's get the sheets out." Lay her on the table. Nature takes care of everything. Meanwhile the guy's at the phone; "Send an ambulance up to Central Avenue and Ninth Street to the firehouse. A woman's going to deliver a baby soon." "Okay." She's on the sheets and the baby comes out. You wrap it up and you hold it there. You don't cut the umbilical cord. Let them do it. They came up and took it.

*　*　*　*　*

Sussex and Dickerson, there's a one story church. We pull up. This guy, he's going to commit suicide. "You son of a bitch, jump. You're going to commit suicide. Jump. Why didn't you go down to one of those buildings down on Broad Street and jump." The captain said, "Don't excite him." "What? Don't excite him." One story building, he's going to commit suicide.

*　*　*　*　*

We have an alarm on Thirteenth Street and Central Avenue in the middle of the block. I see smoke coming out of the basement. "Oh, shit. We got a working fire." I stretch from the corner. We roll in. We go down in the basement. Dirt floor, guy dug a pit. He was barbequing a pig.

Deutch: A man was standing on the ledge on the eighth floor. We had a spare apparatus, a real old spare. Thank God we put the net on because we had a lot of equipment all around that we didn't put on, but we had the net on. It was just a signal five really, just for our crew, which was bad because it was just us manning the net and one Policeman. He jumped and he landed hard, but being the man weighed only about a hundred pounds, he lived. I think he broke his pelvis. I was in a very bad position on the net on that one with my back to the wall. It was in the apartments up the street on Court Street. You're looking backwards up. He didn't want to live, but he did.

When we got the call for a woman jumper, they knew a little more about net catches and they sent in an eight. We had over ten men on the net. The woman was a little heavier. She was hanging from the sixth floor bathroom window. An Army officer ran up and held her hand because she must have decided to change her mind. When we got into position, he flung her out. She landed very heavy, but she also lived. Jimmy Nolen was the captain on both those catches. Right after that they took the net away. It was too dangerous.

* * * * *

Let me tell you about the ship fire. We climbed up the gang plank on that to fight it, a hold fire. We had four lines going into that hold and it was a chemical burning, so we had masks on. I forget what mask we had down there, but it wasn't a good mask because I helped Chief O'Boyle put his on. He had them going into the hold to fight this fire. When we came off of that ship, we walked off it. It was even with the dock. We almost sank the ship. We had to stop throwing water on. That was a three alarm fire, bad fire. It was just a big hole and the hatch cover was open. It was just throwing water in there. It was not going out because it was some chemical. I think a New York fireboat came over and they cut a hole in the side and really hit it with a line. But it was taking so much water we were told to stop.

Denvir: Well, when I was at Eleven Engine, it was around the time of the riots. In the tavern a couple of doors down, there was a black guy. He was from the Sheriff's Department. He shot a guy in the leg. A big crowd started. He came up to the firehouse. These people were all around the street and they were screaming. There were a couple of guys in there, "We're going to riot tonight. We're going to burn, burn the city." Two cars with two or three guys, detectives, they came in and went "boom" right into the crowd. Bam, bam they grabbed three guys, boom into the car. They took off and everything broke up. They knew who the agitators were. They grabbed them and everything calmed down.

McGee: One time we went to a box alarm. Pete Sheridan was on the back step. I was the captain. I think it was somewhere around Central Avenue and Norfolk Street. It was a box alarm, so naturally we were about ready to pull up. I says, "Well, let's wait a second. Let's look around." We see this fellow leaning out of the third floor window and Pete says to him, "Fire?" You know, asking him the question. The guy goes "Fire!" wrong inflection. Now we hear, way in the back ground, we hear "Fire!" and everybody starts bailing out. There was no fire.

Wall: Interesting thing happened at the Academy on Jersey Street. I guess Public Service still owns the right of way in between. Friday afternoon, everything happens on Friday afternoon. I get a phone call and it's from a disgruntled employee of Public Service. He said, "There are containers of cyanide in that building. They've been there for years and it's a totally unsafe situation. I'm calling the newspapers on it. I'm giving you guys the heads up because I have nothing against the fire department."

At that time I knew the Safety Engineer over in Public Service in Harrison. I call him up. He said, "Holy Christ, I don't know. I haven't been in that building in years I don't know if anybody has." "I know it's Friday. Would you do me a favor? Would you come over and let's take a look."

We went in the shed and there are these large barrels. Like you would imagine beer came in during the prohibition era. Real large wooden barrels lined apparently with plastic with a heavy, couple of mils thick cover. Each barrel weighed nine hundred pounds. There were over a hundred barrels in there. This is in this leaky shed where if kids ever broke in there you'd be in deep. So, I immediately give Public Service a violation notice. I know about it. You have to do something about it, right? The safety engineer understood that. He said that came from when they used to burn coke over in Harrison and from it would come manufactured gas. Somehow the cyanide was used as some sort of mitigating factor to reduce sulfur in the manufactured gas. Harrison originally manufactured gas before natural gas came in.

This stuff had been laying there probably for twenty years. Now, how do they get rid of it? They can't transport it the way it is because now it has to be in hermetically sealed drums. Finally, Public Service some how or other cuts a deal with some panning company down in Georgia. They agree to take it off P.S.E.& G.'s hands. They'll handle the transport of it. They had to get EPA and DOT permission from every state they passed through from Jersey to Georgia. I never thought they'd do it, but they did it. One bright morning eight or nine big flatbed trailer trucks show up with a crane and all this other business. With State Police escort, they load the trucks. They brace these things like they're bracing an atomic bomb and off they went into the sunset. Never to be seen by us again.

Freda: I got a call one night that there was a bad accident on the Turnpike. We didn't know what we were getting into. On the way there, the Down Neck units were calling in saying traffic was completely blocked up. They were traveling with the traffic. I don't remember the entrance they were getting on, but their route would have been with the traffic to the accident site. The traffic of course was completely blocked up and they couldn't get through. It was a very foggy night. I remember that. My driver says, "You know Kearny just opened up a brand new entrance. Let's get on at Kearny and if the traffic's backed up, we'll go against traffic and go up the Turnpike and get there." I said, "All right." So we found this entrance, just opened, the one off 280 in Kearny.

The guy taking the tolls thought we were completely nuts bringing this big fire rescue truck, going against traffic, but there was no traffic. It was completely stopped. I remember getting on the Turnpike and it was so foggy that we couldn't see. So I decided for safety sake that I would get out in front of the truck with someone else with our port-a-lites because you couldn't go fast. It was totally blind. It was that foggy. We would walk and guide the way so we wouldn't hit anything or run off the road. You couldn't even see the lanes.

We were walking up the Turnpike for about ten minutes and I saw two headlights coming at me. When they approached we waved. He saw our light and he slowed down. It was a sixteen wheeler. He came around the accident. We let him go by. I was concerned about him hitting us. But he was traveling very slowly because it was very foggy.

Shortly thereafter we came upon one of the most awesome sites I've seen on the fire department. I remember very plainly coming upon and seeing a Kearny fireman with a little hose line sitting amongst this pile of wreckage that ran for several miles, trying to put these fires out. It looked ridiculous, but that's all he could do. There were cars and trailer trucks mixed up together on fire, tires burned off them. It was a horrendous sight. We couldn't get past the accident. I wanted to get deeper into the accident. What we decided to do was cut the aluminum center divider so we could go on the other side of the highway and travel in the undamaged lane. So we could get into the accident site to see who was dead, who was injured, whoever needed help.

What happened after that, we got up the road. It was awesome. There were people lying all over the place. I encountered a man without a head. I encountered a car with burnt skeletons in it. Families we helped because of these trucks and cars crashing. It was an utter mess. I came upon one that stays in my mind. There was a fellow sitting on a pile of debris that came out of the back of his trailer, sitting on the top of debris waiting for help with his belt on his leg and his hand under his chin resting. Deader than a door nail. He had no leg and he literally bled out in a sitting position like that. I remember saying if one of these people, spectators ran over and put a tourniquet on his leg they probably would have saved him. But people were literally afraid to go under there because there were tankers. There were trailer trucks with hazardous cargos. You didn't know what was going to happen. There was one that was carrying hot asphalt that went over and got on one of the drivers, who they found several weeks later because the man with the hot asphalt ran into the marsh and jumped into one of the creeks. Those creeks all lead into Newark Bay and they found him a little later on.

Most of the people were beyond our help. There were a lot of dead people. We did come across a man in the cab of a sixteen wheeler who was trapped because he rear ended another car. He was totally pinned there. It took us literally two hours to get him out of that truck. We didn't have the Jaws of Life and stuff like that then. To make a long story short, we did a lot of first aid. We helped as many people as we could. We searched the whole area and then went back to quarters. We did a lot of work. We were the first unit on the scene. I know we did some lifesaving first aid on people who we stumbled on. It was very fast. We hit people. Do what we had to do, move onto the next person. Up to the time we got stuck with this guy trapped in the truck and practically used every piece of equipment on our truck to get him out of the cab.

The Rescue Squad was the first unit on the scene outside of that one lone engine company from Kearny. We were there through the whole operation, continually working. Never got a commendation. Nobody ever mentioned us. We never appeared in any paper, periodical or anything and we probably without exaggeration did more work than any unit there because everybody else was trapped in traffic. They couldn't get to the accident.

Miller: We had buffs that used to come from all over the state just to ride with Ten Engine and other companies. We would ride one and twelve, two piece company. We had a fire on Elizabeth Avenue. A two and a half story frame, it was vacant, fully involved. We made it a three oh five because we knew we could put the damn thing out. We had a two piece company. We could stretch all we wanted to. We had guys with hooks and axes and we put the damn fire out. It didn't take us that long. In an hour and a half we were back in the firehouse. It felt good. These guys would stay the weekend. They would say goodbye to their wives and they would come up Friday night and stay with us until Monday.

Smith: Now one time I was up on Prince Street before they had knocked all the houses down, right across from the firehouse. They had a three alarm fire up there. I pulled up on the corner. There's a tavern on the corner. There's a hydrant there. There's a guy in front of the hydrant and he wouldn't move. The Chief was down there going, "Water, water, water." The wagon goes down. They stretch a line off. So, I said, "Okay." I got in back of the guy's car. I put it in low, low and I drove right up on the sidewalk. We had the rear hook up. I pulled out, hooked up. This guy called for the Police. The Police come down. The cop says, "What's the trouble?" I says, "This bum wouldn't move. Look at what's going on up there." People were killed there. "Oh." So, he gave him a ticket. I said, "What are you getting him for." He said something about, "Failure to comply with the motor vehicle statue of the State of New Jersey." So, I asked a friend who was a deputy chief in Newark. And he says, "Oh, he got him. That's an automatic five hundred dollar fine."

Dunn: I was fairly new as a Battalion Chief and we had a ship fire in Port Newark. The Fifth Battalion Chief was handling the fire most of the day. Around ten o'clock at night, they called in to give him a break and brought me down. I always remember standing on the deck of the ship with the captain of the ship, like I knew what I was doing. Having extensive fire burning underneath us and not have any ability to know what to do next except to stand there. The ship kept burning and we kept throwing water on the ship. Decisions were being made with Walter Kidde, they used high ex foam on it. Another company was there talking about using nitrogen, to pump it into the ship.

It's quite an ironic thing to be standing there in an unfamiliar situation, two o'clock in the morning and have no idea what you're going to do at the next step. Is this thing going to blow up, sink? What we knew we couldn't do was fight the ship fire because we just couldn't get down below the deck. We were standing at scuttles and portholes throwing water. It was running out of the sides of the ship so it wouldn't sink, but as far as getting into the ship and trying to fight the fire; it just wasn't possible.

After I went back the next night, Walter Kidde came in, covered the cargo holds, and pumped high ex in. What I found out without doing anything, in five days the fire went out. It didn't take anybody taking any beating. Nobody had to go into the smoke. We didn't jeopardize any fire personnel in unfamiliar and closed, confined spaces. That there were other technologies available in fire suppression other than putting a mask on and inch and a half line and trying to fight your way down. Putting men into what I would consider a death trap type of situation. That if you let some time go by and you have some people who know what they're doing from outside agencies come in, that there is knowledge and technology out there that can make our fire suppression a lot easier.

I see that applied more and more as we go into the era of haz-mat; where one of the things they talk about all the time is instead of taking quick and fast action, step back and take a look at it and say, "Is there another way, an easier way, or a better way to handle the situation," which might be doing nothing. I always reflect that back to that ship fire because the ship was smoking away and we were all saying, "Let's go beat up that fire." The different companies were coming in saying, "We go down there and knock the heck out of this fire." You found out that cooler heads prevailed and the smoke didn't do any more damage than was already done to the cargo. By keeping the ship tight, we confined the fire to the cargo hold where it was and the technology did work.

I try to apply that when we go to some of these haz-mat situations where we are unfamiliar with different chemicals. You find as a Deputy Chief coming in a little later, after the initial actions, you come in with a cooler and a different point of view. You can take a more objective view and say "Well, they tried what I probably would have done if I got there first, but I'm not first now, now I'm fourth in line." You realize if things didn't work you change them and one of the options that we have is to back away from them, which we never did before. You can also relate that to abandoned building fires and things like that. We still go in and knock the heck out of our building fires, but there are also times when the men don't like it, but you just say, "Back away from the building. We will use deck guns and nobody will get hurt."

So as I reflect, I place a lot of that back on that ship fire where I found out that, even with all the resources at my disposal, I didn't know how to handle a situation. There were more cool heads there that prevailed, particularly the Navy people who were there, who were familiar with the incident and said "We can do this and this and it will work." They were right. I try as I go through my career, always try to keep that perspective in mind that what we would normally do at first, if you come back and take a second and third look at it, you certainly change your *modus operandi* or the way of operations to make it safer for our people, so we don't get people hurt unnecessarily.

Belzger: Occasionally, at Seventeen in the summer when you were on the book the neighbors would come in to be treated for cuts and burns and so forth. One time, it scared the life out of me, I'm on the book and the doorbell rang. I opened up the door and a guy says "I'm hurt." I looked at him. He didn't seem to have any physical problems. I says, "Well, come on in." He comes in and he had an axe stuck in the back of his head. I sat him down. I hit the bell to get the captain down and we called the Squad. I don't know what happened to him.

Garrity: We had a general alarm and a two bagger at the same time. During the two bagger, a woman dies. She had gone back into the building, who knows how. After we fought the two bagger with four buildings, we got the other one. I was exhausted. My ass was dragging. I was huffing and puffing and the Rescue Squad had taken up. I just wanted to get a hit of oxygen just to get some breath back in. I see Leroy Smith from EMS. I say,

"Leroy, you have a rig set up with oxygen?" He says, "Yes, go around the corner." So I go around the corner and they have the big rescue rig there. The guy says, "What's the matter?" I say, "I just need some oxygen, I'm just winded." "Why don't you go into the truck," he says. "We'll take care of you."

So I go into the truck and he says, "Why don't you take your coat off. As long as we're giving you oxygen, we'll take your blood pressure." So they take my blood pressure, they're giving me oxygen. The guy says, "Well, as long as we're taking your blood pressure, why don't we put a cardiac monitor on you." They put a cardiac monitor on me. He guys says, "You know we ought to take you to the hospital." I says, "That's it. I ain't going to the hospital." So now I start a row with EMS.

They bring the Deputy over. Chrystal says, "What's the matter?" I say, "They want to take me to the hospital. There's nothing wrong with me. I'm tired. I'm forty-eight years old. I'm beat to shit and I want to go sit down somewhere." "You have to go to the hospital." "There's nothing wrong with me." "You have to go to the hospital." All right, so I go to the hospital.

They bring in the doctor. The doctor looks at me, looks in my mouth, looks in my nose. What do you think they see? Soot, lots of soot. Like years. Took a chest x-ray. Bring me back. Now they're giving me an I.V. They did blood gases. Do all this. The doctor comes in to me and says, I got bad news for you." I figure I've got a tumor on my lung or something. "What's the matter?" She says, "You have chemical pneumonia. You have to go to the burn center." I says, "Lady, there's nothing wrong with me. I'm old, I'm fat, and I'm tired." She said to me, "You have to go." I think Mooney was there from the Rescue Squad. I say, "Jimmy, what are they doing?" "If that's what they think it is, you had better go." "There's nothing wrong with me." So they say, "Well, we're transporting you up to the burn center. You have to go." "If you don't go, you're going to be put on charges." "Okay, I'll go."

So, I'm waiting. I'm lying on the gurney in the emergency room and in comes a volunteer ambulance squad from Livingston who was sent down to get me. They come in and say, "Who's the fireman that's burnt?" Then they say, "Who's going to the burn center?" "Oh, I am." "You're burnt?" "No." They look. "You have to go." They come in with the gurney. "No, I'm walking. There's nothing wrong with me. I'm telling you this." I wouldn't get in the gurney. I said, "If I'm going, I going to walk." So I have an IV bottle in my hand, put my helmet on my head, my coat over my shoulder, and I walk out to the ambulance. When I get to the ambulance, they want me to lie down. "I ain't lying down. There's nothing wrong with me." Get up to the hospital with red lights and siren. I told them, "Turn the lights off. We're not in a hurry here. There's no emergency." "Well, you know you're getting . . . ." "Just don't do that. I don't want to get run over because you're in a hurry to get somewhere."

We get to the hospital, the burn center. "Get in the gurney." "I'm walking." Still have the helmet, the coat. You go in through the air locks. You go down the hall, you make a turn, go through another set of air locks, and then you make a turn into the burn unit itself. As I make the turn, there're four people with surgical masks, cap, gowns, booties. And they look at me. They say, "What's wrong with you?" "I keep telling you. There's nothing wrong with me." "Well, we have to examine you." They had given me the x-rays to bring with me. So they're looking at the x-rays. They said, "Whoever processed these x-rays, they're backwards." I don't know what that meant, but they were backwards.

They called the head of the burn center to come out at five o'clock in the morning to look at me. This guy comes out. He says, "What's wrong with you." I say, "Nothing." "Then why did they send you here?" So I go through this whole scenario. Tell them the whole story with all the adjectives and all the carrying on. I'm not lying in the gurney. I do the whole number on them. So he looks at the x-rays and he looks in my mouth. He says, "Your mouth's full of soot." I say, "I'm not smart enough to keep my mouth closed when I'm pulling ceilings, so of course there's soot in my mouth." He says, "Go rinse your mouth out." I start spitting it out, spitting it out, spitting it out. Finally I get it all clear. He looks at me again. He takes blood pressure. They had done another set of blood gases while I was there. And they look at the x-rays again. The guy says, "You're right. There's nothing wrong with you." This cost the city somewhere in the vicinity of four thousand dollars.

Haran: We had a ship fire. It's quite a long time ago. It was burning for a few days. It caught on fire while it was in port and Chief McLaughlin was the chief. I can remember him. I believe I was still in Salvage at the time and so I was only new on the job. It burned for several days anyhow. I don't think we really had that much experience in fighting ship fires. The technology has improved in firefighting over the years tremendously. We had these Chemox masks. We had guys with more balls than brains going down into this ship. I believe I was one of them at the time. We had a lot of good men and the ship burned for three or four days down there. Eventually it went out.

I don't remember where it was from. I think it might have been even a banana boat, if I'm not mistaken, unloading bananas. I do remember you couldn't stand on the deck even with your boots on because the deck was so damn hot. We didn't have anywhere near the tools we have today, metal blade cutting saws and that type of thing. We did have an acetylene set up on the Rescue Squad. We had them in salvage, too. But they were only small, portable tanks, like the small resuscitator tanks today. They only lasted maybe a half hour to fifty minutes. For something on a ship fire like that, you would need something for a long duration. But they used to call in outside agencies at that particular time to help us out also.

Cahill: We had a fire at 3M Company, an explosion down there. This is in the daytime, we were rolling in and we can see people burned, in shock. It was like the walking dead. Everybody is running out. But we didn't have the training for hazardous materials. We went dashing in. Not even knowing what they have there. It was very difficult, too, to find somebody from the company who could tell you. They all seemed to disappear, management, engineers. They didn't know. We had no idea what we had. It was an explosion, so it was well vented. It almost blew itself out.

What I do remember at that fire was seeing a block wall come down and seeing a pair of legs sticking out. We wanted to pull the guy out. All of the sudden there was a leg in our hands. We got the guy out, but he had lost that leg in a prior explosion at 3M. So this guy was on his second strike. I don't know if he retired that night or not. If he didn't, he didn't learn anything good.

McGovern: We had a fire in a slaughter house Down Neck, turned out to be three alarms. We got down there. There was this large barn with beef on the hoof. The place is rolling. Captain Kosar of Four Truck said, "Sure going to be a lot of dead cows in there." We ask, "What do you mean?" "They're just pouring water on from ladder pipes." We go around the back, cut the gate, and go inside. There are hundreds, hundreds of beef cattle in there, standing there burning with the roofing and hay burning all around. They're burning alive, "Moooo." It's dark out; it's like two, three in the morning. So we opened the overhead doors, went in, and started slapping these beef cattle on the ass trying to get them out of there. They wouldn't leave. Half of them were burning. They weren't going to go anywhere. We finally got them moving and Bitter, who is a frustrated cowboy, he's swinging his port-a-lite. "Hey! Yeah! Go!"

In the mean time they're all shuffling out the door in a big herd now and I'm cut off. The fire's behind me and the cattle are in front of me. The only way I can get out is to go over the cattle. I had visions of climbing over these cattle's backs. So anyway after the fire Dolak, who's Deputy Chief at that fire, asks for a report of actions, a second or third alarm report. Bitter writes, "Arrived on the scene. Found hundreds of panicked occupants in a state of distress burning inside this building and due to the language barrier we could not communicate with them." He wrote this report up like it was a rookery with Spanish speaking people. "We wound up evacuating hundreds of these non-communicable panicked residents." He typed this up. Dolak walked around with that report for years, kept it in his pocket. He'd say, "Here, you want to see a rescue. Here, read this. Here's a rescue, hundreds of people." He loved that report.

Carragher: We had the airplane fire down at the airport. I think it was a 707. The plane was parked on a ramp about five o'clock in the morning. It was on fire. The Port Authority dumped foam all over the outside, but it was an inside fire. And they said, "We're going to go get foam." So, then we had to set up lines and attack it like you would a house. Eventually it burned a hole in the roof, probably a ten by ten hole in the roof and vented itself. We went in with inch and a half lines, washed it down and put it out.

*   *   *   *   *

I just was reminded of a fire last week by Chief Cody and Chief Smith. The practice fire we had at Avon and Rose when they came on the fire department. They were the recruit class that had a three-story frame, six-family duplex house lit up for them. Chief Drew, who at the time was in charge of the Arson Squad and Training, loaded this place up with varsol, straw, accelerant, and all that and lit it on fire. All the families are lined up on Avon Avenue. The street is blocked off. The wives and families are all watching and this house took off. These guys are up on the second floor and couldn't get out. I was in Rescue or Twenty Engine. I forget which one then. But we were told, "You're not going to do anything. You stand by and watch." After about thirty seconds they said, "Grab some lines and get in and put this fire out." The guys were trapped on the second floor, had to get ladders up to them. The wives are screaming. The families are all panicking. Our new hose goes up into the building. What are we doing here?

*   *   *   *   *

There was another building over around Court and Lincoln. Three story frame again and they were going to demonstrate, one afternoon, high expansion foam. It was brand new. They wanted to sell it to the city. I think Drew may have been chief again and he boarded up all the windows on the first floor and the basement. Again he did a good job with the varsol and everything like that. The guy from the factory, the factory consultant, said, "Chief wait a minute. We're going to put a cellar fire out. We can't put a three story frame out with this thing." Drew says, "Ah, you want to sell us your product? Let's see how good this stuff is." He lit this and this house took off. The foam put the fire out in the first floor and the cellar, but it didn't put the second and third floor out. By now we had all the companies surround and drown this big bon fire.

*   *   *   *   *

Orange and High Street used to be a railroad depot. There used to be a meatpacking place on the corner, Swifts Meat, behind that was a coal pocket. I would think the coal pocket was probably about four hundred feet long and probably three, three and a half stories high and say fifty feet wide. They used to bring the railroad cars up in there and drop the coal into chutes. It was all wood, a wooden framed building and for years when I first came on the job they always talked about the big one. That was going to be the biggest one in the city, when that coal pocket went, if it ever went.

Well, one night when I was a captain in Six Engine it did go. We came over on the third alarm. This thing was fully involved, top to bottom, front to back and nothing could be done. We came in on a little street up above High Street. I forget the name of it, where Northern Oil is. I remember Twelve Engine being on the corner and Dominic LaTorre may have been the captain. He says, "We have to get those tanks covered." All the oil tanks are steaming and boiling from the radiated heat. We're talking maybe two hundred feet away. I said, "Okay."

We had gotten a new rig in Six Engine, a Ward LaFrance. It was a diesel, the first diesel in the city. You could pump with that in low gear. You could move in pump. It had that road-ability in it. So, we pulled up and I said, "All right, let's try this." We got in there. Mike Fitzpatrick was in there. He was in Three Truck, I think. They started pulling off hose. I said, "We're going to put the deck pipe to work and see what we can do. But pull off about four extra lengths on each side and hook it into the deck pipe now with the extra slack." I think Freddy was driving. We put

Costigan up on the deck pipe and I think it was Wiggins on the booster. I told Twelve, "Give us all the water you got." We advanced on the fire and drove up until we got that with the deck pipe and put the whole thing out with the deck pipe from the one side. We were a good distance away, but we needed the protection from the booster. The rig was starting to get a little steam off it.

That's how we actually put that fire out. Went right up with the rig and knocked it right down. We had it in road and pumping and we had Twelve Engine pumping us with the supply lines. We just pulled up. The pumps we had were only for the booster line to cover Costigan on the deck pipe. That's how we advanced up there and with the pressure we had and everything, we got it right on the fire. It was a surface fire. It was heavy timber, but it wasn't like a dwelling where it's in deep and ingrained where you can't get to it. This was all surface. So when you started wiping it down, you're hitting it. You could see the whole thing go right down.

* * * * *

There was an attempted suicide one day over on two forty-four Chadwick. It's an L shaped building. The parking lot's on Bergen Street. There's a guy outside the fence on a roof ready to jump and there are a couple of cops up talking to him. We snuck the Snorkel in behind that building that day. Teddy Harazda was the operator. He, Bitter was the captain of the Rescue Squad, and myself went up and nailed the guy. The guy never saw us coming. We got up right behind the guy. When he saw us, he turned and before he could do anything we had him. The cops and we had him.

Finucan: The funny stories I can remember. I can remember we had these kids. It wasn't that long ago because they were going to Spencer School.

Everyday these kids would be walking past the firehouse. I'd be sitting there in my chair. I always sat out front. They'd say, "Hey, Mister fireman, there's a big snake in that sewer down there." The same kids are telling me every day and it was going in one ear and out the other. Little kids were saying, "Yes, he hisses at us every time we go by." So, sure enough, I went off duty, but it was in the paper the next day that they pulled this twelve foot boa constrictor out of the sewer on Boyd Street and Mohammad Ali there. I saw that in the paper and I looked at the address. I said, it was about a half a block up from the firehouse and this is what the kids were talking about. So, there was a snake in there.

* * * * *

I always remember going to a fire at a hotel on Lincoln Park Christmas Eve. A guy set a fire in an artificial fire place, one of these cardboard fireplaces, sets a fire in it. Burned out his apartment, caused everybody to have to flee the building on Lincoln Park. It wasn't a really bad fire, but it was a signal eleven. I can remember standing there with my pad and pencil because I was first due, taking the names. Who the tenant was, who's this. So, the guy who set the fire, I happened to be talking to him and I asked the guy, "What's your name?" He says, "My name is James X. Brown." So, all the sudden out of left field, this woman comes with a big stick. It must have been two inches in diameter. She bops him over the head, knocks this guy out cold. She turns to me and she says, "His name is James Brown and you can leave out the X. He started the fire." He burned her out. She came out and she said, "His name is James Brown. You can leave out the X." And old James Brown without the X is laid out on the ground, bopped over the head by this woman.

* * * * *

I can remember a guy I gave first aid to on some nameless street corner somewhere. I was a novice at the time. This guy is lying on the corner, alcohol all over his breath and everything. I said, "What's the matter?" He says, "Oh, I don't know. My stomach hurts." So, I says, "Let me see." So, we open up his shirt. I look at his belly. There's this big thing hanging out of his belly. I'm looking at it and I'm thinking it's some kind of a growth, like it's a wart or something. What happened is he was stabbed. Stuck a knife in him and they pulled the knife out. His intestines came out with it. There was very little blood because the intestines just plugged the hole on the way out, but the knife had pulled out these intestines. And this huge thing is hanging out. I'm saying, "What the hell is this?" Who comes along but Leroy Smith from EMS. He took over. He said, "This man's been stabbed and those are his intestines."

Pianka: I think one of the scariest things that ever happened to me was at a fire on Belmont Avenue just before Clinton on a Sunday morning. I remember being on the third floor fire escape in front of the building. I had a wooden hook, set it down next to me. I go to put my mask on because I could see the fire in the back. We're going to go in there. You could see it across the hallway. Put my mask on and somehow I must have tipped that hook. It leans over the edge of the fire escape and starts to head down hook first. And my heart just jumped out trying to grab this hook and my eyes followed this hook down. I'm looking beyond the hook and Billy Hielman is down in the entryway hooking up a hose line, bent over, with his back like a big target. The thing misses him by a foot. He just looks over and goes back to what he's doing. Meanwhile, I'm up there. I'm a basket case. I almost fainted because I thought for sure I was going to kill him. I didn't know it was Billy Hielman at the time, but I'm thinking to myself, "My

God, I can't live with that." But it's just one of the stupid things in this job. I never did that again.

*　*　*　*　*

Another thing in Five Truck, plane crash on Elizabeth Avenue and we had this old piece of junk Pirsch that can't get out of it's own way. The whole alarm flies up Elizabeth Avenue. We putt up Elizabeth behind everybody else and we get flagged down, down on Watson. The guy says, "Hey, there's a plane crash back here. All the guys went past it." It was a mail plane. Two guys got killed. It wasn't a huge plane. It was a small plane. It was behind the old Weston Industry company on the railroad tracks back there. They were taking off and they went down. No fire, the two guys were dead. The only thing I remember was the poor guy's boots laying in the track. I said, "My God. How the hell could that happen?" Both of them were still strapped in their seats like a hundred yards away. The guy's boots were in the middle of the track, both of them together. That was freaky. I said, "Wow, how did that happen?" Just his boots and he's lying in a ditch shoeless. He was strapped to his seat shoeless.

*　*　*　*　*

Another time we went to Fourteenth and Bruce. Half the time we were going there it was either a fire or a first aid. Some poor old guy died. You have to picture this. Woman says, "Oh, my grandfather died. I don't know what to do." "Well, we'll call the ambulance." "Oh." She's all nervous. We go up there and sure enough the man's laid out on a bed and it's dark in the room. The woman went out to the front, to the kitchen and she's all nervous. Me and Billy are sitting there with our helmets and Eddie McCarthy comes up. He looks at us. He says, "It looks like you're keeping vigil here in a funeral parlor." And sure enough, I look around and I says, "Gee, you're right." There was even a candle somewhere burning. This poor guy's lying there. Said, "Yes, we're keeping him company until the ambulance arrives." It was just one of those freaky nights.

That morning we sleep in. This was a Sunday morning. That was our first night. Billy and I are still in the firehouse. Some guy had a seizure out front, so we go out there and help the guy. I think it was just before our relief time. Go home, come back that afternoon. Somebody comes running into the firehouse. "Hey, somebody hung themselves in the projects." It was the same guy who had the seizure earlier in the day. I said, "Holy shit." Because both of us recognized him right off the bat. So we cut him down, tried to help him. No good. We were leaving there. The cops were saying, "Hey, who's the guy who cut him down?" So, we looked at him. "We did." "Don't you know it's a crime scene? You can't do that without us." "Get the hell out of here. The guy's hanging there." "Yes, well there are seven people in the next room." I said, "Well, what do you think? You think they all murdered him?" Anyway, proceed that night, a couple of more deaths.

Monday morning I go home. I remember I took a bath because I just wanted to relax. I was shell shocked. We were fighting fire and all kinds of nonsense the whole weekend. I never forgot that. That had to be one of the toughest weekends I ever experienced on the fire department. We just got our heads handed to us. Needless to say, we were young. You bounce right back. That's it. That's part of the game, but it stuck with me.

*   *   *   *   *

We had a little two bit fire on Littleton Avenue. Some guy is laid out on the back porch. So, we say, "Hey look there's a body over here." We're looking at him and Sparky, Mark Hopkins, says, "Ah, he's dead." All of the sudden out of that darkness you hear. "Oh, no I ain't." Everybody is like, "What?" I'd say you ain't.

*   *   *   *   *

When I was at Five Truck, we're going down Clinton Avenue. We hit a bump. The wheel pops out on the tiller, so I hit the buzzer. I hit the buzzer and they stop. Those are the kind of things that you remember. Putting a ladder up to a window; going up the ladder and then looking back and realizing that the ladder is twisting because the truck that you just came up from is rolling down the street. What happened was it was on a slight incline. It wasn't properly chocked. What I think the driver did was he drove into the curb thinking that the curb would chock it, but it didn't. The brakes didn't hold. And it started to roll. As it rolled, the ladder stayed in that window because we were in the window. It didn't give. But as it was going it started to twist. As a matter of fact, Mastroeni was just about coming up because you could see it was starting to twist. I said, "Frankie, what the hell is going on?" He said, "I don't know." And he came scampering in. The lucky thing was it jumped over the curb, hit a tree, and stopped. It went a few feet, but enough to twist the aerial.

Stuff like that or having an old '50 Pirsch. Went to a fire, had a spare 1950 Pirsch. Put the ladder up, but the ladder's moving. It moved by itself. You couldn't lock it. This was stuff that was in the field. People complain now, you wouldn't believe the truck.

*　*　*　*　*

We had a project fire, I got the tip. We're at the door. The door is still locked. It's smoky in the hallway. You know you have a good fire in there. You can feel the heat and all that. You can see it puffing around the door already. I kneel down right in front of the door to put my mask on. The line's charged and something caught my eye at the bottom of the door. Something was moving. I thought it was a bug. What the hell is that? It was a dog's nostrils. I put my mask on. I open the door. Smoke comes pouring out over our heads. The dog runs out. It's a big German Shepherd type of dog. It goes about three feet from me, squats down, and takes the biggest dump you ever saw. He was so scared. He shit right there. I said, "Wow." Then he took off and we put the fire out. I'll never forget those two nostrils. There was like a gap. I said, "What the heck is that?" I never saw anything like that.

Another dog story, we go to Irvington for an assist call. Anyway, Irvington has a good fire going. Larry Krieger's in Six Engine with us. We jump into this back yard. We're stretching a line back there. This dog, ferocious looking dog comes running at us. I said, "Oh my God." Larry said, "Don't worry, he ain't going to bother us." He comes lunging at Larry. Ba-boom, he punches the dog. The dog runs away. "Geeze, Larry, where did you learn that?"

*　　*　　*　　*　　*

Another animal story, we go Down Neck. I'm back at Five Truck now, and Richie Bitter is in the Squad. Go down there. It looks like a warehouse. It turns out to be a stable, a holding place for cows. It's going good and then to get to the entrance there's like a corral. There's a whole bunch of cows in there. There are about fifty cows in there. So, we're all with the hose lines. Everybody's afraid to go in there. So, Bitter comes over. He says, "What is it with you guys? Don't you know what to do with cows?" He opens the gate, takes his helmet off. "Ya-hoo!" I said, "Okay." So then we go inside. We go in there and there are like haylofts. Like on a mezzanine level. We're putting these things out. As we're putting it out it's darkening down, but it's hot in there. You realize there're cows in there. "Ah, Jeeze." I'm bumping into it. "What the hell was that?" It was cows. You could hear them breathing. They were lowing real low. I said, "Oh my God." They weren't doing anything. So we just went on putting this fire out. I said, "Boy these stupid animals are really dumb. They don't have enough sense to get out of the fire." All of the sudden you hear, a-ba-boom. They fell over. Now it's like, holy shit, we better get out of here. These things fall. They're going to kill you.

We all backed out and later on everything cleared. These poor animals, they were standing there. Their backs were burning and everything. Finally they were just starting to die because they just couldn't take it anymore. That was a memorable one. And then to top it off, Chief Bitter writes the second alarm report and he wrote it as if the victims were human beings. He writes a long narrative telling, they were trapped. They couldn't get out. They're backs were burnt terribly because they had to stand there. That was a good one. That's something you don't see anymore. You don't see livestock in the city anymore. Or any city on the east coast like that.

* * * * *

We had a fire up in the Burg and we came back. I had jumped off the rig and walked into the firehouse. Meanwhile, they're backing the fire engine in and I walked across the apparatus floor from the side where the engine is to the Chief's side. In the back there, there's a radiator there and a drier for gloves. I'm taking my gloves off. I'm in the process of putting the gloves on the drier and I hear a crackling noise. At this point the engine is already in and the door is coming down. I hear the crackling noise. "Is that the radiator?" All of the sudden I feel a burning sensation on the left leg on my inside thigh and I'm facing the radiator. My instantaneous thought is, "What's going on here? Is the radiator blowing up or something?" But another couple of milliseconds and it dawned on me. I said, "That's gunshots. I've been shot." Holy Christ.

So now I drop everything. I run. I start running toward the house watch room. I'm going to the door, but I don't make it because I'm shot in the leg. Sparky's coming out and I just fall down because it's painful. It's quite painful. I says, "Sparky, I've been shot." He says, "What?" I says, "Please, I've been shot in the leg." "What are you talking about?" "Pull my pants off. Pull my pants off." So, he pulls my pants off and sure enough, in my thigh there's a little spot the size of a dime, blood just welling up, not flowing freely. He says, "Holy Christ." In the meanwhile, Kevin Killen, who had been upstairs, came down and he saw me laying in the back and all the commotion. His first thought is, "Holy Christ, they ran George over." This is the mentality at work here. "They ran him over."

Now Chief Kinnear, Davy Kinnear is there. Davy went through the riots. Davy Kinnear is our chief now. He was the Battalion Chief when Mike Moran got shot, same thing, in the leg. He remembers. Mike died. He says, "Holy Christ." Kinnear comes back, sees me shot, and his thoughts were, "Oh my God. I went through this before." So he says, "Put him in the gig right now. We're going to take him down to the hospital. We're not even going to wait for EMS." Meanwhile there's all kind of radio traffic. Billy goes out into the street. Like what's going on? Right after they shot. He looked like Pugs McGoo and he's standing in the middle of the street. I remember Sparky saying, "What the hell's he doing?" He's standing in the middle of the street and he's looking back. "Hey, get in here before they shoot you."

So, they pile me into the gig, take me down there, and sure enough everything turns out all right. The bullet's lodged in my muscle, in my leg. It didn't hit any arteries, nothing major. Thank God everything's okay. There are a couple of days I'm the hero for the day, all the fame and glory. People are saying, "I heard your name on the radio." "Yes, I'm alive." All's well that ends well. I was happy to be alive.

We pieced what happened together afterwards. When I walked across the apparatus floor the chief's gig wasn't there. There's a hold up across the street. There was a cop in the bar and the bartender was ready for anything with his own gun. Ready, if anything happened. Four guys come in. The bartender knew right off the bat. Something was coming down, that these guys were up to no good. So, as these four guys came in, they sat down. The story I got back was before they even did anything, the cop and the bartender took their guns out. These guys realized and started to run out the door. The cop and the bartender are pumping bullets out the door. I'm in the wrong place at the wrong time. Bullet comes across, through the plastic overhead door on the chief's side and catches me in the leg. After this happens, the chief comes. Ray Frost is driving. Later on, when I had healed and came back. Ray and I checked where that bullet hole was. If he had pulled in or if he had been in the process, either the chief could have been hit or Ray could have got it right between the eyes. I mean it was just one of those quirky things. And the fact maybe, that it hit that door, slowed it down enough where it dropped and hit me in the leg too. Rather, if the door had been open it could really have done some damage. Could have caught me higher or could have killed me. Who knows?

It was bad luck that I got shot, but it was something that was probably inevitable because of all the guns in the neighborhood around that firehouse. I mean another incident somewhere around the same time. We were backing in and sure enough one guy's shooting at another and the guy being shot at is running toward us. Now, we don't know what to do. Run away from this guy, shield him. We're backing in. We run in. All right come on in. Get in here, but everybody hide. Close the door. It was that kind of stuff. And you were going to get caught in the crossfire.

* * * * *

After I got shot, I'm out three, four months or whatever. Come back, I'm back not a week. We're on a day trick. We just finished cleaning the rig. A woman comes in with some guy and the two of them are arguing. This and that, he's beating her up or something and she's pissed at him, so we're separating the two. I said, "Look pal, get over here. Move aside because we're going to kick the shit out of you if you keep this up." I turn around, this woman had a brick in her hand. She goes to hit him, whacks me in the face. I get so pissed. I was so upset over this. I made the Union file charges. We're going to court. Gerow says, "Look, we can only push this so far." I says, "All right, I'm cooled down." I says, "We'll go before the judge." The judge says, "If she apologizes, will that be enough?" I said, "Fine, but you have to understand. I was very upset at the time." He says, "Oh, I realize that, but I can't send her to jail." She was a mother. I didn't want her to go to jail anyway at that point. That night I could have ruined her. I wanted to destroy her. But that's the kind of stupidity that you got involved in. You didn't have to look for it. It found you. It was there, all over the place.

Five Truck was the same way. We had Gershenbaum's next door and all the guys hung out in front of there drinking. They would come into the firehouse looking for sandwiches and stuff like that. One day they called us out, "Hey, come here. You see Charlie's legs, something's wrong." So we go over there. It's loaded with maggots. The guy had a wounded leg. He had a leg wound from somewhere and they didn't take care of it. I guess he was lucky that the maggots were there. They were eating the infection. When we looked at that, I'm like, "Holy Christ." I never saw that before.

A lot of times they'd call you out. "Hey, Joe's over across the street in a car and he ain't moving." You go over there. Joe's as stiff as a board. He'd been dead there for God knows how long. But that's the nature of the people in the neighborhood. It's tough. It was a tough place and different people reacted differently. To me it was just like, "Hey look, this is a miserable place and they were in the misery." I feel pity for them. It's too bad. It's just too bad that you have to live this way. I'm not a religious person. But I do know that whatever spiritual feelings I could have had are being satisfied by this job. I'm doing good. I did good in my own way. I fought fires and I helped people. Nobody else was going to help them, but we were out there, just you and that guy who said "I ain't." But we were there to make sure he was alive. We picked him up. "Hey, pal, get up."

Ryan: I remember opening a hydrant on hydrant inspection. A drug dealer came running up because that's where his stash was and it went floating down the street. Another time we opened it up and there were baby sharks, dead ones, in the hydrant, all these fish came flying out. "Wow, that's pretty cool." But the normal stuff in the hydrants, bottle, rocks, all the variety of debris that you could imagine.

* * * * *

Life in the firehouse was interesting. Made more so by numerous first aid calls. We had plenty of walk in first aid calls, knifings, stabbings, shootings, delivering babies, you name it. They have called us for everything. And people always called us for everything. You really got to the point that you were running all the time. At the time I went over into the Rescue Squad to try that out, we were the fourth ambulance in the city. There were only three ambulances serving the whole the city at the time out of Martland Medical Center. University system EMS had not been set up at that time. So, if three ambulances were busy, we in the Rescue Squad would take the call. We were the fourth. We were running all the time.

I delivered three babies. It wasn't something you directly considered being firefighting, but it was really different. I was happy to deliver the babies on three different occasions. That was another high point, great fun and then eventually bumping around I did run into one of the babies on a number of occasions because they were right on Fourteenth Avenue. It was neat. It was quite an experience. The second one, the one lady, she was probably in her latter thirties and my first question to her was, "Have you ever had any babies before?" She said, "Honey, this is my twelfth." "Well, you know a lot more about it than I do, because this is only my second." All three babies were delivered without any problems at all. That was a true pleasure too.

*   *   *   *   *

We all became real good at first aid, depending on where your firehouse was and what the neighborhood consisted of, whether it was a volatile neighborhood or what. But there were very few confrontations actually between citizens and firemen because they knew that you were there to help them. It was well known that Six Engine, Eleven Engine, Ten Engine, Twelve Engine, you got real good at bandages and you did first aid. The alarm system was intact. The street boxes were going. People would pull the box for anything. I remember pulling up on South Orange Avenue and Thirteenth Street. There was a fellow there; obviously an inebriate and he wanted to go to the hospital. "Why? What's the matter with you?" "I'm drunk." "Take the Thirty-one Dover Street. Call yourself a cab." I notified headquarters and they sent the local John Doms up and corralled him because he was getting rather frisky.

*   *   *   *   *

When I was a Captain down in Ten Engine, we had a fire in the building next door. It's going pretty good on the second floor, coming out the back. This man comes running out. "There's a woman on the second floor! She needs help." I go up the stairs to get the woman and she's only got one leg. I see this shadow up there standing in front with the flames in the background, silhouetted against the flames and she hopping down, on the one leg, down the hallway. Never did find her leg, but got her out. That was fine. Same piece of property after the building's torn down. One of the guys in the neighborhood comes in and he says, "The man's stuck on the wall of the building next door." I say, "Yeah, how'd he get up there?" This is a partially demolished wall and there were all sorts of cement sticking to it. You could actually climb it. So sure enough I go out and there's this guy about half way up this three story brick building. He's sitting like spider-man going up the building and he's hollering and screaming. There's a whole crowd gathering. A fellow came up, "Captain, Captain you got to get him down. He's scared." I say, "Well, he got up there. He probably can figure out how to come down." "No, you got to get him down. You don't understand. He's got hydrophobia. He's afraid of heights." That's a true story.

* * * * *

I bailed out of a couple of places. I had one, ran out of air on the third floor of a place, Fourteenth Avenue somewhere. Just dove down the stairs. We were stuck. We were really stuck. We dove. I was with Pete Petrone on another job over on Peshine Avenue. We crawled into the third floor and the thing flashed. We just dove. There were guys coming up from the second floor. We're on fire. We landed on top of everybody.

Me and Petey Maloney, we jumped out of a second floor. I don't know how Petey did it. Petey walked on a little tiny piece of wood across the front of the building. But we went into the second floor, report of a woman trapped up there, couldn't walk. We got up there, trying to make a grab before the line got in there, taking a chance. There's nobody there, searched around the room. All of the sudden the smoke starts banking down and the flames start to roll across the ceiling. It starts getting real hot. You could tell it was in the walls. It was in the cockloft. This is not good. As the place flashes, I ain't gonna burn. I'm going out. I'll take the broken bones, but I'm not going to sit up here and burn to death.

Al Taylor was driving Nine Truck. He saw where we were. He swung the ladder out, extended it. Joey Garrity was the captain. Al Taylor saved my life that night. I really feel that. I didn't know where I was going. As I jumped out the window, I got maybe, I dove about three feet and Nine Truck's ladder was right underneath me.

*   *   *   *   *

If there had to be a favorite fire, this is right up there. We received a telephone alarm of fire on the first floor of the Sheraton Hotel right off of Port Street. I responded down there. Upon my arrival, confirmed by people coming out and security coming out that there was indeed a fire. I called a second alarm because it was a high-rise building. The upper floors, we were getting reports, were rapidly filling up with smoke. So we evacuated the entire hotel. The fire was on the stairwell on the first floor. Not much of a fire, but it did fill up the top floors with smoke and there was smoke through out the building. The fire consisted of several mattresses, a food cart, and other rubbish that was right at the bottom of the stairwell. Intense heat, it was like an oven going in there, but it got knocked down real fast. We were very concerned about people being trapped on upper floors with all the smoke that as going up there and obviously, there was considerable smoke.

At the time there was a convention of the Far East Nurses Association in the hotel having their dinner. They had just sat down to dinner. Fortunately, there weren't very many people in the rooms. There was a family re-union from the Carolinas, a large family re-union, several hundred people. And there was a wedding going on at the same time. They had all sat down to the meal. Most of the people in the hotel were business people, who were in and out, or were directly involved with these three large parties. As I said the fire went down rapidly, but we couldn't allow anybody back into the building because of the heavy smoke that was in there. Anybody who was subject to respiratory problems would have trouble. So, I had gone through my tank and I came out.

What the hotel management had done was set up several tables outside in the driveway area. They had brought couches out to the outside and all three parties were in full commencement by the time we came out of the building. So, we had several hundred oriental nurses. We had several hundred people from this very large family re-union and a large wedding party, all three parties merging into one. The hotel people had set up tables with food and drinks, soft drinks. They kept the ice coming and they kept the canned soda coming.

As you'd go walking out of the building the oriental nurses would basically jump you. One on either arm and they would slam you up against Fourteen Engine and take a picture with you. They got poor Father Raught like that. And there were two on each of his arms. He had a big smile on his face.

When the Director showed up, he quickly looked around. His jaw went a bit slack. Got him into the main part of the hotel and he turns to me and he says, "Joe, I never saw anything like that in my life." I says, "Neither have I, boss." Because of the prolonged period, they wouldn't let the people back in the building, but they had their food, they had their party and it was on the front lawn of the Sheraton Hotel. Probably had four, five hundred people up front, having a party while we're putting this fire out.

After the fire was out, everybody was in a great festive mood and thanked us for putting out the fire. It was a pleasure. They were genuinely happy. The little bit of irony on this was that the Far East Nurses

Association has a reunion every four years someplace in the United States. One time it's on the west coast, next time it's on the east coast to accommodate where ever they're coming from. The last reunion of that organization was in Los Angles and at the time of their last reunion four years previous, they had the large earthquake in Los Angles. They come to here and they have a hotel on fire.

So, it was really great. The people were fantastic and panic was averted by all means. We got them all out. Had no one hurt. It took several hours to clear the smoke from all the upper floors. And it's really remarkable and very memorable occasion. In this business of working with disasters and seeing people at the worst times of their lives, it was really refreshing. They made us feel very welcome and how appreciative they were that everyone was out and the party kept on going all night long. We were invited to stay for the parties and of course we had to go back to the firehouse. Some of the single men I'm sure were tempted to join in the festivities, but we had to go back to work.

*   *   *   *   *

Haz-mat, had some great haz-mats. We had some twenty-six thousand gallons of gasoline at a refinery on the ground. That was pretty fun. Responded on a report of a gas leak, this thing's going up in the air from a six inch pipe. Looked like a fountain in the middle of a town square. "Wow, look at that." The air on Doremus Avenue away from the scene tested as high dangerous and as we moved into the yard, the fumes were so dense it was low oxygen. It was an amazing fire. The Port Authority had two crash trucks out. That was a new run thing. Had some pretty good haz-mat, other stuff, poisons, tanker trucks rolling over.

Connell: While I was at Five Engine an alarm came in for 411 Wilson Avenue. It's right after the overpass for the railroad, there's a chemical company there and there's a fire in the back. It was New Year's Eve. It was four below zero and they told me, "You have to stretch a line and back up Eight Engine." I stretched a line through the factory building, out the back door, all around the loading docks to where the fire was to back up Eight Engine. There was a pit in the ground I didn't know about. It's all ice and snow covered. I guess it had to be ten feet deep and ten feet wide. When I was half way across it, the ice broke and I fell through. The whole thing is like slow motion. I can remember the water starting to trickle down my boots. I'm saying, "Gee, it's going to be cold tonight." Then I felt it coming up around my head and I said, "How deep is this?" Then I remember going under. I felt the water going down my boots a little faster. Training Academy, they always told us, with these three quarter length boots, they're like anchors. They fill up with water. They'll take you right to the bottom. There's no getting them off. You're dead. So, I hit the panic button.

Somehow or other I fought my way back to the top and there was a bar that was running maybe a foot below the water line that went across the whole pit I was in. My arm just fell across it like dumb ass luck. Tommy Joyce had seen me go in. He was the first one to come over. He got me out of it. That was the first time I almost died on the job. That will always stick in the back of my head.

Then about a week after this happened I had a strange smell in the liner of my helmet. The uniform I was wearing and everything else had like grease stains. Chief White came one day and said, "Go down there, buy whatever is ruined, and they'll pay you for what was damaged." So, I went out and bought a new helmet, liner, work uniform, underwear, the whole routine. I went down there and they handed me a check. About six months later, Chief White came around and he starts asking me a bunch of questions about this job. So, I figured maybe I'm going to get in trouble for taking money off this company. He wouldn't answer any questions I asked him. So I went to the union and I asked them how come there's such an interest in this job that's almost a year old now. It took them a day or two, but they finally got back to me.

What it was is the State was investigating. This company was in the business of disposing of toxic materials. What they did was they'd fill up tanker trucks. Every time it rained, they'd go on the Jersey Turnpike, open the valve, and drain out as they drove down the Turnpike. And they wanted to know if I had any ill effects or anything else and what kind of pit I fell into. I never found out exactly what came of this, but the company went out of business a month or two later. And I was never able to get a firm answer on what actually I fell into. This was before there was anything known as haz-mat.

*   *   *   *   *

When I was on High Street, Four Engine on the third tour had a fire next door, three kids died. They couldn't get the overhead door open, so the engine couldn't get out into the street. But the captain used his head. He put it into pumps inside quarters and stretched inch and a half off, using his tank to attack the fire. He made statements that if the door was opened, they could have saved the kids and everything else. All that's debatable; I wasn't there. I didn't see the fire conditions. From what I understand happened, they were beyond being saved, but again we embarrassed the city.

Bisogna: At Five Truck, we had a fire where a woman was severely burned. She was unconscious and they were carrying her out. I think Kenny Miller had her legs and he was going down the stairs first and Ray Stoffers had her under the shoulder. It's pretty hard to carry somebody down a flight of stairs holding them down low like that. She must have got out of Ray's grasp and she falls down the steps. And Kenny, who's the captain, looks at Ray and says, "You stupid bastard." She comes to and says, "I'm sorry fireman." She's apologizing for getting dropped.

*   *   *   *   *

This is a job where a lot of funny things happen. You look back through the years. I had a naked woman get in the cab. We're going to a working fire. Tommy McDonnell's the Captain. I'm driving the hook and ladder up Avon Avenue and you could see the glow in the sky. Eighteen's on the scene. They've got a working fire and we turn the corner and there it is. I mean it's lit up. It's like a candle going three blocks away. There's a taxi stand there at Clinton, right at the turn there where the triangle is. This naked woman, nothing on but sneakers, about thirty years old, runs out in front of the fire truck and throws her hands up. "Stop, stop." Now Tommy is going, "Run her over. Run her over." But I know I'm driving and I'm not going to run her over. The interesting part is you could see there's a fire and there's a naked woman.

She goes around to his side of the truck and I start to go. She comes right back around the front again because the truck didn't jump out. You know it starts to go slowly. So she waves her hands again. I look and she says, "He's trying to kill me." There's a cab driver sitting there laughing. He's in his cab. He's looking at me. He's laughing. She must have gotten out of the cab. I want to see this. She comes around to Tommy's side again. He goes to open his door to say, "Lady." She gets in. She climbs over him. Now I'm driving. Well, she's going to the fire. I've got a naked woman sitting next to me "He was going to kill me. He was going to kill me." Tommy's looking at me and I'm looking at her. So, we get to the job and Ray Frost is Chief's Aide at the time. I said, "Ray, I've got a naked woman in my truck." He looks in the cab. He looks at me like, "What are you guys doing?" I said, "Look, just get a blanket. Bring her a blanket." And that's what she needed. She got the blanket and was on her merry way.

Ricca: At Five Truck they gave us a truck that they put together. The aerial was from old Three Truck and Chief Toriello bought a White cab, not white color, White brand name. Captain McDonnell just about fit into the cab so you can imagine if I was acting how it was. But you had no contact with the people in the jump seat because there was the glass of the cab and then there was the canopy where they had the bench seat. You rode backwards. So, Richie Bennett's acting, I'm driving. We get a fire somewhere on Route 78 and I'm tooling along up 78. I'm not sure who was tillering. We past the last exit in Newark and I turned to look at the cab because Ray Stoffers knows that area. And he's plastered up against the back window yelling, he's face is contorted. Well, I look at Richie. I said, "Richie, I think we better shut the siren. Ray's mouthing words. He saying we're not getting off until Millburn now. So, we quietly made the U turn in Millburn. Chief Hestor was the chief and he's looking for us on the air. "Truck Five where are you?" And we said, "We're caught in traffic." It was like two in the morning. There was no traffic.

* * * * *

Tillering, backing in at Five Truck, the driver used to go as fast as he could. For the width of the doors it's a miracle that we never did more damage than we did backing into quarters. But there were a few times we took the doors out.

Two quick stories, I'm up at Nine Truck and I'm driving. The captain and I didn't see eye to eye on everything. So, the box comes in. I thought it was Bergen Street. It's an old Pirsch and on this old Pirsch you sat in the ladder with a canopy you had to clear if you had a fire. The ladder extended maybe eight feet behind the tiller canopy. Bob Langevin was tillering. I make a left to go to Bergen Street. The captain takes his helmet off and is pulling on his hair, which he didn't have any of. "Kerrigan, Kerrigan." He also lived on Kerrigan Boulevard. Well, being fairly new at driving, fairly new on the job. I throw it into reverse and put Langevin through the door, the overhead, up to the tiller cage. His eyes are like three miles wide.

On another occasion, I think it was Mike McCrone tillering. Tony Peters was driving and Rob Schimpf is the captain. We're trying to back the rig in. Remember, we're a new crew. He's got it in reverse and the rig is bucking. And Schimpf just sat there with his cigar. Schimpf's head is going back and forth like the little dog in the back of your car. After about, no exaggeration, fifteen minutes, they couldn't get this rig in if they pushed it in. Schimpf got out, politely slammed the door. Went and wrote the book up. Went up to the bed and the guys are still out there trying to put the rig in.

But they were some of the nightmare stories of tillering. You had to jack knife the truck before you raised the ladder and you had to do it with the cab. Guys used to think they could jack knife by turning the tiller cab in, but it wouldn't give you the same point because you had to over steer to your opposite side of the fire, reverse the direction of the wheels, come back, and actually push the point of the truck in towards the fire. So, guys who tillered thought they would help jack knife by turning the wheel, but it wouldn't work out.

The nightmare story of Five Truck was when they left without the tillerman on the Second Tour. They didn't make it too far after they took the doors out. I think they ruined the steering box on the tiller cab. It was a mess. That was with the White cab where you can't look back and see what is going on. At the time I don't even think there was a horn.

A hysterical moment was to see Five Truck on the second tour going down the street with Eddie Camuso in the back with a boom box and head phones on. That didn't last for too long before he was told it couldn't be done. But you were in your own little world back there. With the White cab we couldn't communicate because the speaker never worked right anyway. Everybody had a different sign. Ray Stoffers used to motion with his hand and you knew it was a working fire.

*   *   *   *   *

One time we were going down Belmont Avenue and I think around Clinton Avenue. I was tillering. The truck stopped and a woman jumped in. We continued onto the fire. As we get to the fire, I see Ray Frost who's driving the Chief, running with a blanket. Captain McDonnell gets out and now to my night accepted eyes at that time because I was still rubbing the sleep out when we stopped, a woman gets out with nothing on but sneakers. Ray Frost covers the woman and takes her into the gig. It happened like it was a movie; that it was meant to happen. The write up from Captain McDonnell was the tale of the unknown jogger.

What had happened was she was a hooker; she got undressed. The guy kicked her out of the car and she was running around Belmont and Clinton Avenue. But to see the rig stop and her just hop in like she was supposed to be there was unbelievable. She sat in the middle of Tommy and the driver, which was really hard to do because there was no middle seat, so they were all squashed in the front.

Chapter Four: The Price

Kinnear: Deaths were tragic. Not that you could have done something because most deaths, you couldn't have done anything. It was there and it was done, a lot of times, before you even got there. Sometimes you felt, "Yes, maybe I could have done something different." I think more with children, young kids, or babies. When you saw them and especially when you saw where no one was around. The parents weren't around or the parents just left them or the parents took off and saved themselves and not the kids. It affected you, but I really never felt a sense of any kind of guilt or anything. That I should have done more or anything like that. You would think "maybe if" the alarm had come in a few minutes sooner maybe they could have been saved. In a sense it's sadness about it. But I never had a sense that it was my fault or the company's fault or anybody's fault. It was something that happened.

F. Grehl: I was in a backyard and there was supposed to be somebody in the third floor of the fire building. They were going up the front with hose lines. I went around to take a look at the back. They had all wooden back porches. So, I thought, "Third floor. I'll try and get up there and break open the door. I'll holler for a truckman to come and force open the doors." I could hear this person in there hollering. So, I tried to get in. I couldn't get the doors open or anything. The next thing you know "poof." It came right out the third floor windows, the whole third floor. I was on that third floor. Where do I go now? I can't get down. I can't jump. But fortunately the houses were close.

* * * * *

I think you remember things that you were in command of more. How many people are up there dying. You hear them screaming. Do I send people in there? I know it's too much jeopardy, but I know the decision is made. They're going to die if I don't get in there. So, what do we do? We concentrate all of the streams on the stairwell. Try to get in there. There was the night Kevin Killeen heard the screams up on the second floor. We tried the stairway and the stairway started to collapse. So I said let's go through the second floor windows in the front. We poured streams in there. I think he got into about the first room and it just got so bad we had to pull out. There was the baby right there. I can remember that fire as clear as could be because we could hear the screams, but we couldn't get there.

Wall: I was Captain at One Engine and we were called to, I think it was a fifth alarm behind Saint Anne's Church on Sixteenth Avenue. We're on our way up there and we get diverted to a fire that turns out to be a second alarm on the corner of South Orange Avenue and Bergen, in one of these U shaped apartment buildings. Commercial occupancy on the first floor and I think four floors above it, apartments. Larry Caufield was the Battalion Chief. We're way out of our district. As soon as we pull up he said, "There's supposed to be people trapped on the third floor." So, my crew stretches a line up the fire escape into the third floor and the building is clear. We have little pockets of fire here and there. We're going room to room. The floor was sound. I see a little a bit of a fire on a doorway.

Suddenly the truck company opens a ladder pipe up into the cockloft and drops everything down around us. We can't see, blacked out. I can still see the fire on the doorway. I remember Vinnie Delarant and Bob Dougherty were on the line with me. I said, "Hold the line here and let me pull that, so something doesn't come down on our heads." I was walking across this floor before. Walked to the door, turned to pull and I dropped right down the burned out stairway. I figured it was a hole in the floor, so I put my arms out to grab the beams, but there are no beams.

I know this part sounds farfetched, but I felt like I was falling for a long time. It was almost like one of these *out of body* things people talk about. I felt like I was falling for a long time. To a point where I had a light in one hand and the damn Halagan hook in the other, I told myself, "You better get rid of these." and I let them go. I tried to pull myself up into a ball. Figuring like a paratrooper, I'd land and try to roll. Suddenly I landed in the basement. I can't move. I can move my arms, but I can't move anything below my waist. I feel around. I feel I'm on something, so I try to roll off. I drop into about two feet of water. I don't know how I did this to this day, but I saw light and I crawled to the light. With my helmet I broke out windows and I crawled out into an alley. It was like a depressed alley between that building and the parking for the Howard Bank. The Howard Bank was on the other corner. I couldn't move. I couldn't yell. I was winded.

Finally the same clowns who had opened up the pipe into the attic spotted me and they came down. I said, "I broke my back. Get the Squad here." Meanwhile, Vinnie knows I'm gone. He shuts the line down. They come down looking for me. They find my helmet. They find my tools way the hell over here somewhere. They don't find me. They're digging through all sorts of rubble. What I had landed on was stacks of black Moslem newspapers. It was a black Muslim newspaper print shop and these were papers they hadn't sold. There were high stacks. They broke my fall.

They take me to Presbyterian Hospital. That night it looked like MASH. There are all the guys from the fifth alarm. So, I'm in a gurney. They couldn't even get me into a room which ends up being fortunate because Doctor Artie Devlan was there. He was a buff who rode with us at the Squad. He's the first guy to see me. "What happened here?" I said, "I think I broke my back." He said, "Well, I'll get you right into the operating room." Took me in, x-rayed me, comes back. He says, "Good news and bad news. You fractured your spine, but it's a compression fracture of the first lumbar vertebrae. And I'm almost positive that by tomorrow or the next day you'll get your feeling back. Right now your body's protecting yourself and you're paralyzed. But the best I can say is there's no damage there. There's inflammation. As soon as we get that reduced, you'll be okay."

That was on Good Friday. So, I asked, "Don't notify my wife. I'll call her in the morning." In Newark they never mention your name when you get injured, right? Some stupid radio mentioned "Among the injured, Fire Captain from Engine One Edward Wall seriously injured. My wife doesn't hear it, but my sister in Linden hears it. Calls Dorothy up and says, "How's Edward?" Dorothy says, "I don't know. He didn't get home from work yet. He's fine as far as I know." "No, he's in the hospital. He's seriously injured." So now, when she comes to the hospital, she wants to kill me. My sister found out before she did.

Three days I was out of the hospital. Never wore a brace. Devlan said, "Don't let anybody convince you to operate on your back. It would do more damage than good." Just needed to do isometric exercises and keep the weight off. It bothers me occasionally; if I put on ten pounds then I know it.

I had surgery two, three years ago, so they put you through this MRI and the doctor said it would show any injury, fracture, whatever. So, he said, "Mr. Wall I have good news for you. The cancer has not spread, but you have the worse set of bones of any patient I have ever seen." I said, "What do you mean?" He said, "You have stress fractures in both shoulders." He said, "You look like your spine was fractured and both knees. What did you do for a living?" I said, "I was a firefighter and we get those injuries." You know hauling hose; you get the stress fractures in the shoulders. I fell a couple of times on my knees. I guess, little fractures show up here. So, he showed me the MRI. You see like a little hot spot where the fracture is.

When I fell I had this Janesville coat on and it shredded. I don't know what the hell I hit on the way down, but it looked like a cat had shredded my arms. Janesville actually replaced the coat. I got a free a coat out of it.

Deutch: We used to get fire deaths. We might get nine people burned to death in a rooming house. But as far as commercial business went, I think everything was well run. It was some of these slum areas. The fire would get such a good start, you'd lose big families. We had the body bags. We'd put them in and nobody likes to handle them. You'd feel it, for a while you feel bad about it. I remember having six bodies down off Elizabeth Avenue, Sherman Avenue. We had them all over the place. You don't forget it. Most of those people were dead before we would get there. I have to say that.

* * * * *

There was the time a roof came in at the end of Plane Street down near Court Street. I was ordered up with an axe to cut holes in the floor because there was so much water. Before I could get the axe in, it came in. Bill Carragher, Chief Carragher, was trapped under the roof and he was under water. We got the roof off him and pulled him out. I think he'll remember us taking him out. I could just see his feet. He was going to drown. We got him out in seconds. You get the strength. Three of us just lifted the stuff off him.

Freeman: I remember my first death. It was up around Fourteenth Avenue. We went into the back. I don't think there was that much fire, but I remember we went in and I thought this was a little doll on the bed, but it was a dead baby. I just couldn't get that in my mind that this was a baby. It was charred. I saw a guy sitting at a table once dead. He had been drinking and he was just sitting there just like you're sitting or I'm sitting. I guess he was asphyxiated, but he had been drinking.

* * * * *

There was another one where they lost twelve people. We didn't get that fire. That was at night. They called companies in up there to sift through the ashes for human parts. I remember finding some human parts myself. I think I found an ankle bone that was not attached to a body, just part of it. That was awesome. You're sifting through all this stuff and you're finding pieces of bodies. That was awful.

But it's just part of the job. It just happened and I had no remorse. In fact I began to question myself as to why I didn't have remorse because I know a lot of guys that do. A lot of guys don't like to look at death. But it didn't bother me. It bothers me more now than it did then. I think about it more and deeper than I did before, but not to the point where I'm remorseful or I didn't do a job.

McGrory: Defeat isn't the right word to use in describing the feeling firemen had when there was a civilian death at a fire. Because I think most of the time when we went out the doors, we tried to do the best we could. So it wasn't a matter of defeat. You hated to see anybody die in a fire. It seemed to be a waste. The death could be right across the street. You didn't want to see anybody, especially children. Firemen often say, "Yes, well they were dead probably before we even left the firehouse." It was true on many occasions, but still the men have to put up some sort of defense for themselves. Because you can't operate and take everything and let it get to you. Sometimes you wonder how these guys can be in EMS all the time or how an undertaker could be an undertaker. We did the same thing.

Human beings will set up their own defenses. But I think, in my experience that every time we got there we tried to do our best, to do a job. If there was a life at stake, men took extreme chances with their own safety to do something positive about that. So, I think on a whole we did a very good job. You didn't want to see anybody hurt or injured.

I remember a young child who was burned. There was no fire. She got burnt in a flash over, something in the kitchen in the morning with grease or something. She ultimately died, but I can still remember that child sitting on the stairs at six o'clock in the morning on a nice Sunday. She was burned terribly. She was still alive just sitting there in shock, but that child died. There was nothing we could do.

Marcell: I went to many a fire. I went to a fire where eight kids died at one fire on a Sunday morning and the following Saturday six kids died at another one. Then the following Sunday as we rotated at home four more kids died.

Freda: Let me tell you about the worst experience that I vividly remember. I was in the Rescue Squad no more than a month. We had a box come in for a paint company off Broadway. We went to the box and there was a fire, but what apparently had happened, there was a spillover of tanks and the spill landed all over a worker. The worker was burned severely. He was lying off to the side. He was burnt to the point that his skin from head to toe, with no exception was totally black. His arms were stretched out. I guess because of the charred skin and the muscles, his arms were frozen in that position. We couldn't get them back in.

Why I remember it is because he was alive. He wasn't talking. I don't know what his conscious level was, but he was alive, he was breathing. To see a human being like that, I've never seen someone burnt that badly and alive. I felt so bad for him. I remember thinking, "I wish this guy would die." Because I knew he was going to die and I wished he would die soon because this is ridiculous. We had trouble getting him on the stretcher because of his arms and getting him in the truck. We had to actually shut his arms and crack it. Otherwise he wouldn't fit into our truck. We were transporting in those days. We brought him to Saint Michael's and I think he lived several hours at Saint Michael's before he died. But to see a fellow human being suffering like that was such an awesome sight. I never forgot that.

*　*　*　*　*

The other things, the children we saw that were dead or severely injured. That bothered me. And there's one other case that had a profound effect on me. It had nothing to do with a fire. It was a case that we went on. That a woman was being beat up by her husband on the third floor apartment, a brick apartment. And to escape her husband she ran and jumped out the third floor window. Her little child who was three years old ran and followed the mother out the window. It was very dramatic to think there was a bond between this mother and child so strong that the kid literally followed his mother out a third floor window. Fortunately for the child and unfortunately the woman, the woman hit the pavement and died and the child landed on top of the mother and survived. I never forgot that because just to think that the bond between a mother and a child was that strong that a child would literally jump out a third floor window to follow his mother out of danger. There's no fire. There's no danger, but the mother was being beat up by the husband. He wasn't beating on the child. He just followed his mother out. I'll never forget that.

Dunn: I was a Captain at 12 Engine a short time. I had a bang on the door type of alarm, where we opened the front door and the smoke was in front of the firehouse, eight o'clock in the morning, eight-thirty in the morning. You look at it and you realize the resources that you have available to do fire suppression, probably the best firefighters around at the time. Across the street you have a heavy fire condition, but instead of it being fire out the windows, it's a heavy smoke condition. You get into the building and you do your firefighting tactics which are inch and half, the aerial to the roof. It was in April, probably '65. When the fire cleared we had five fatalities, five children age one, two three, four, five right across the street from the firehouse.

You look around and you look at your thousand gallon Class A Pumper and your senior aerial truck with five of the most experienced firemen in the world and all the resources at your command to prevent what happened and yet, because at that time there were no smoke detectors, a delayed alarm type of situation developed. Five people died for absolutely no reason.

Belzger: We saw an awful lot of deaths when I was on the job. It seemed like every time we went to a good working job, we'd find a body. I had several experiences with it. Probably the last experience was Milford Avenue. We got a call about eleven o'clock and Twenty-nine Engine was out doing something. We beat them in. We got first water and it was a one room job. We knocked the fire down. We found six kids in there. I remember running over and taking the baby out of the crib. She had the black marks around her mouth. I knew she was gone, but you try to give them mouth to mouth resuscitation. Here I am holding this little girl. I'm on the porch. I'm trying to get her to breathe again. The mother came down the street. She was a Puerto Rican lady. She was scooting down, then she found out it was her house. When she found out I had her baby in my hands. She goes, "What are you doing to my baby?" And I said, "I'm trying to bring it back to life." She screamed. It was a horrible, horrible thing. It always stays in the back of my mind, that picture, mid-day like that.

Later on I found out that she was down at the corner store buying milk and bread for her kids. She left a nine year old in charge of all six of them. She had one right after the other I guess. She met a woman from Puerto Rico and they started talking and she took too much time. We figure one of the kids, probably the nine year old, was playing with matches, but the smoke markings were down about twenty inches from the floor. It really got going and why they didn't leave the room, I haven't the slightest idea. I guess they tried to put it out or something and became overcome or something like that and that was it. But there were a lot of instances like that. I used to hate carrying the body bags out.

Guys were some firefighters in those days. They were tough, really, really tough. You couldn't see anything stopping them. I'll never forget, Hillside Avenue, we had four kids die, little babies. They looked like little dolls, bloodless dolls. All white no blood in them and guys were giving them mouth to mouth all the way out of the fire, all the way into the ambulance, all the way until you get some other kind of respiratory thing on their face. You just see guys sit down and cry because kids, they have no control over things. They are innocent victims.

Carragher: Fires with deaths at them, you get tired of fires with deaths. We had so many. We had the one over on Bloomfield Avenue or Park Avenue where the guy stabbed his mother-in-law, his wife, and his sister-in-law, put them on the bed and set the house on fire. We went to the fire. We put it out and find three people that were burned lying on the bed with their shoes on? We said, "What the hell is going on here?" We started checking and on their chest you see little welt marks. Let's call the cops. Well, we sent them to the hospital, but they were all stabbed to death. It's only in the past six months that they caught the guy who did it. This fire happened in 1982. The guy was a professional soccer player, Scot Bollenhague is his name. He took off to South America. They had him once before about three years ago somewhere down in South America and he escaped. But then they just caught him about six or eight months ago. He's back in the country now awaiting trial for that.

*   *   *   *   *

I know the one that I remember always is the one on Halsey Street. I was in the Rescue Squad then and the roof collapsed on us. We were in the building down there, three guys from Twenty Engine and three from the Rescue Squad. A couple of guys broke their arms and a couple broke their legs. I got hit in the head with the section of the roof. Chuck Deutch and someone else got the section of roof off me. I was in a building under the roof. The first thing I thought when this roof came down on me, I thought I was going to drown, because there was so much water on the roof. That's what knocked it down.

It was a two-story loft building on Halsey Street, down probably around Court Street or somewhere in that area. There was a three story exposure on the north of it and a vacant lot on the south side. Ten Engine came in and put a deck pipe to work on this building. It was heavily involved on the second floor. Put a deck pipe to work to protect the three story exposure. Someone else came next to him put a deck pipe to work. And someone put a ladder pipe up.

Meanwhile we came down with the Rescue and Twenty. We figure, "Hey, we don't need deck pipes. We'll put this thing out with a two and half." We grabbed a two and a half and in we went with it. We were advancing right through the building, knocking everything down, but the weight of the water on the roof collapsed the roof on us. That's when the guys got hurt, including myself. I got banged on the head, got a bad back to this day. I got a bad back from it and never realized it.

I was maybe about ten feet behind the guys on the tip. They said lighten up. I bent down to lighten up and the next thing I know, I'm laying under this section of roof with water pouring all over me. I thought I was drowning I had so much water coming over me. I had the mask on. I had the Burrell mask on. I said, "Oh my God, I'm going to drown under this." The next thing you know, "Wait a minute. Wait a minute. I'll get you." And I heard Chuck Deutch. Chuck came over and picked up this section of roof and got it off of me. I got up. I see the other guys and I was only about say ten feet from the door. I ran to the door. And they told me to come to the stairs. Jimmy Kennedy I think it was in Twenty. I said, "Get some help. There's guys trapped up here." With this now a couple of guys came up the stairs and we went in and got the other guys out. But we had knocked the fire down by now. It was mostly all knocked down.

Highsmith: Freddy Grehl was the Fourth Battalion Chief at a fire and as we got up there, it was very hot. We got into the bathroom. It was so hot in the bathroom that all the tile, shower curtains, everything had just melted. No fire it just melted. And the tub was full of water. Freddy Grehl touched the tub, "There's somebody in there." We grabbed a girl out of there and passed the little girl on to him. Then we had to grab a lady out and the lady was just flopping around. I had her against my body taking her down the stairs. Her skin came off against my body. What she had done, she had run into the bathroom and filled the tub with water and submerged her and her daughter. Eventually she died, but the daughter didn't.

But it's just things you have to see, you have to go through. You can't think at times like that. You just react and hope. You don't think of your own safety. You just hope that you could do what you're doing and get away and get the person that you're doing it for out.

*　*　*　*　*

I guess my most memorable fire was not a fire I fought. It was a fire I investigated on South Orange Avenue where a woman and six children died. As we got up in there to look around, you could see the woman, what was left of her, in the middle of the kitchen floor with her two babies wrapped in her arms, trying to get out. She was protecting her kids. That was the most memorable one and it was an accidental fire, accidental fire.

It was the most memorable because it took Hector and myself about eight hours to really get down to the bottom of it, because we had to search every hospital in the city. A fellow fled the fire scene. He had jumped to an adjoining roof, which was a garage. The owner of the garage had inverted nails in the roof so that the points of the nails were sticking up to keep people off. When this guy jumped out the window, he jumped down on all these nails. He rolled off of that, fell down to the street, ran across South Orange Avenue, and was sitting up against the wall bleeding from every part of his body when EMS pulled up. We had no clue that this guy was in a fire; that he was taken away by EMS; or that he was in a hospital. We had to question and question people and question people. Finally, we found out in a hospital, "Yes, there was a fellow in here, but he wasn't burned." Come to find out, he was the one who was in the house. He tried to get the people out, the heat got too much for him. He jumped out. Told us where the fire started and everything. That was the most memorable one because we lost so many people at that fire and all the kids. It was just an accidental fire.

I think about it. It's nothing that gives me nightmares or anything like that. If somebody asks me about it, I can talk about it. It's just that I remember that one because so many things happened in the course of that fire. You know, you don't get thanked because you're doing your job.

Butler: Probably the biggest thing and I don't like to think about it because I still look at the injury, probably the accident we had with Eleven Truck. Where the overhead door came down as I was tillering going out to an alarm. The overhead door dropped and was riding on the ladder. I was unaware that the door dropped because the side man used to ride up on top of the fender, holding on by the tillerman. He jumped because he saw the door. I thought he fell.

I am looking down over the side, bouncing the ass end of the truck and the ladder off the lockers on the other side of the floor so I wouldn't run him over. At the time it was after the riots. It was in '72. Steel cages were built over the tiller man. It was the old Pirsch, I was sitting in the ladder. The steel cage hit the wooden door, dug into it. As the vehicle pulled out, the steel cage bent, dug into the door, lifted the door up so we were able to clear out from under it. That's the cause of my crooked finger here. That's the way that happened. I had a concussion, banged up shoulder, cuts all over the face and neck from the glass in the door breaking and coming down. That was about the worst accident I've been in. I've been injured a lot in fires, but nothing monumental.

*   *   *   *   *

Anytime you time you had death at a fire, a civilian, guys really thought, "Oh Christ, how did we fail? What did we do wrong? What didn't we do that we should have done and maybe be able to save this life?" Coming up I had some good officers, real good chief officers. Quite often we'd sit and follow it up, critique it, talk about it. Maybe go back to the scene and look it over again. It was kind of figured that I would say probably seventy-five percent of the deaths in a fire that I was at the people were dead before you probably even got the alarm, let alone arrived at the scene. There was nothing you could do to save them. They were cooked and dead already. You find a death and it's just something, no matter what you did, you weren't going to save them.

A couple of times, you know you made some rescues, they were still alive but died later or something. It's a situation too where you got them out alive. It just happened for one reason or another. You try to follow up on them all. "Chief, what happened? What was the result of the death or something?" He'd try to find out for you. Some of them you hear heart attack. Maybe the stress of the fire or the anxiety of the fire, but it wasn't directly related to the fire. And some were smoke inhalation. They just got too much smoke before you got to them.

*   *   *   *   *

We've had incidents, shitty ones. A couple I pulled out. One on Sixth Street near Fifteenth Avenue I guess, we got there, Artie Murphy and I went up the ladder into a third floor window. We had taken the windows out with the ladder, made a big area and went up in because they were telling us kids were up there. We found four kids. Three of them died. I found one right after I stepped in the window. Artie jumped off the ladder and went to the right. I climbed off the ladder. I went to the left and I stepped on the kid right away. I picked her up, young girl, but very heavy. Meanwhile a couple of other guys were coming up the ladder. I laid her on the ladder and the other guys took her and I kept right on going again. Found a three or four year old kid, handed out. Artie was coming along holding one and dragging one. Got them out, but then the joint really started to light up, but that's all that was there, four kids.

We got them all out and we were told later that two of them were dead when we brought them out. One died on the way to the hospital or something. The fourth one survived. The one that survived was the littlest one of them all. The one Artie had carried under his arm is the one that survived and he found her on the floor in the corner.

The death of kids was hardest. Bad enough to die in a fire, but kids, especially little ones like that are almost helpless. They can't do for themselves what adults might be able to do. You throw something through a window or hang from a window or something where little kids can't do that. It's really tough.

*   *   *   *   *

My first fire death was on Eighth Street and Twelve Avenue. Three Truck was around then and I was working with Tommy Rush and somebody else from Three Truck. We put two ground ladders up to a porch over the first floor because they were hollering kids in the second floor. I looked in the window. You could see the kid, the kid's body. The whole second floor was engulfed in flames. You could see him rigid. You almost saw bone structure more than anything else. The kid was on the bed. You knew he was dead. Hollered for a line, knocked down what we could, went in, and we were able to pull the kid and get him out the window, but half the skin of his body was burnt off.

We got there and we were up on that roof in seconds. That fire was cooking. Here's a kid in a bed. Why didn't he wake up? Why didn't he get to the window? If he had gotten to the window he could have crawled out onto the roof. You don't know who or why, but that was my first fire death.

Knight: A memorable fire was in 1973. It was the one and only time I felt I got seriously hurt. We went to a fire on Summit Street. I was on the first tour in Three Truck. We went to a fire on Summit Street in from Sussex Avenue. We had a row of two story frames going during the day. In with these two story frames, there's a two and a half story frame. We pulled in, the deputy told our company, Three Truck, to try and get into the two and a half story frame and try and get it opened up. Try and get this thing cut off or else it's going to go down the block on us. So I was up on the porch with my Captain at the time, who was Tony DeTroia. I hollered down from the porch. "I got it. I'll go in." Another firefighter from Three Truck, Dick Watson, was with me and we were wearing the SCBA's. I put the mask on and I went up to the second floor.

There was a doorway going to an attic apartment. I opened the door to the attic and the smoke was banked down the stairs in the attic. So I closed the door and I hollered for a line. Two Engine brought a line up and the firefighter on the line was Leo Brochu. We opened the door and he started up the steps to the attic. I started up behind him. We were on our knees in the attic. With the masks on it's hard to understand. I heard him say "Which way do you want to go?" We heard the crackling of the flames. I suggested we start toward the rear of the building because that's where the crackling was coming from. We made the turn and I started feeding some line to him. The attic flashed over.

I was blown down the stairs backwards. I landed on the second floor landing on my back and I knew I was burnt. It blew my helmet off my head. I got up off the floor. My gloves were burnt off my hands. I just got up and went out of the building. I told everybody to get out of my way; I was burnt. I wound up with some nasty looking second degree burns on my hands, my face around the mask. The mask was the only thing that saved me. If I didn't have that on I would have sucked raw flame in. I wound up with a lower back injury. I spent six weeks on injury leave. That was only one of the very few times I was seriously injured. You know, I've had cuts. When you're a truckman you're always getting cut by something. I've had cuts that required stitches.

That was two days before Thanksgiving in 1973. I spent the night in Presbyterian Hospital. They held me for observation and they let me go home the next day. Two days later I was admitted to St. Mary's Hospital in Orange. I had the fire surgeon at the time, who was Dr. Devlin, he thought I had broken my back, but x-rays had shown that I had jammed my tail bone when I landed on the tank. Like I said I put six weeks on injury leave. Finally went back to work, I think it was the beginning of January '74.

When I went back, I was a little scared my first fire after that. It was, you know, it happened to me once. Now you're a little gun shy, but once I got up in there and we started working, everything fell right back into place again. You have the fear. You're always scared. Anybody that tells you they're not scared on that job is full of it. I've never met anybody who isn't scared. You're scared every time that bell hits. You're scared every time you get on that rig to go out. Like I said, you have that in-born terror in you that something's going to happen. But as luck would have it, that's the only serious time that I had.

Prachar: My first job was Fourteenth Avenue and Seventeenth Street, two and a half story frame, second floor fully involved. We pulled up. First due truck, went in, did our ventilation, and that's when I started learning right then and there. When the fire was knocked down, Captain Melody took me, showed me the proper way of pulling ceilings, opening windows, taking the sills off, demonstrated how you take the pike axe, take the pike, into the sill, and pull. I thought it was fantastic, so he gave me the axe, went to the window next to it. Rotted sill, right through the sill, the pike went right into my foot. Scared to death to tell my Captain I was hurt because I didn't want to be known as a pussy. Got back to the firehouse, took my boot off. My boot was full of blood. Never forget it. He just said, "Did you learn a lesson?" I said, "Yes, don't hit it so hard the first time."

*   *   *   *   *

Other memorable fires, quite a few, kids dying. Nine Truck, we had a fire on Tenth Street and Kent, right off of Springfield Avenue. There's a large apartment house there. We came down Tenth Street to Kent, Eighteen Engine in front of us took a line right in the building. We put the aerial to the building. The building on fire was the one behind it. We couldn't see that. We thought it was in the back of the apartment building. People yelling kids are in the building. All we could hear from outside was "Daddy, get us out." Well, the three kids ended up dying. Rescue finally got in, got the kids, but they all died within the next week or so. That was my first real taste of kids dying in a fire. Something I'll never forget. Went home, I had two of my own kids. Just hugged them; played with them all day long. Most of my memorable fires are something involving kids.

Worse time as far as affecting the family is when kids die in a fire. You go home and you grab your own kids. You hear different people say on television how you grab your kids and you hug them. I did it. Kids on

Tenth Street, I went home. I wouldn't let my kids go. My wife thought, "Okay, kids died." See me come home like that. Thought I should have gone to a doctor. That mentally I might not have been there because of that. And it took me a long time to get that voice out of my head. Even talking now, I can hear that kid, "Daddy get us out of here!" You'll never forget something like that. And every time you see your kids, you think how lucky these kids are that they're alive. That they can play hockey like my kid does. My daughter could play softball. That all affects you mentally down the line, I don't care who the man is, something like that never gets away from you. Especially, when you have young kids and you see young kids die. That to me hurt more than anything.

*　*　*　*　*

That day on Tenth Street I felt defeat. Another time on Bergen and Hawthorne, we pulled up; the Police reported a baby and a grandmother in the window. The building in turn collapsed while we were fighting the fire. Those are probably the only two times I could really say I felt defeat. Any other time I felt if I gave it a shot, if had a decent shot and I couldn't do it, okay. But if I didn't give it a shot, then I felt defeated. With the one on Kent Street, the building was too far gone. We could hear them, but we couldn't get in and the one on Bergen Street, when we got there the back was coming down already. So, it wasn't a matter that you could even try.

There were times guys would ask me, "How could you get yourself in a situation like that?" I made a rescue years ago where I walked across a rain gutter to get to a guy in a third floor window. But like I said, a matter of sixty or seventy pounds later, I'm not going to do that anymore. When I was young that was the job. You had to go and get these people. If you couldn't get to them, if you tried your best, then I felt to myself, "I tried." Maybe somebody else came in another way, which happened a couple of times. I went in one way and I was blocked. Somebody else would come in another way and they had easy access. So, if I gave it a good shot, I felt I wasn't defeated. I did my job. No matter what the fire was. How big the fire was. If I gave it a shot, I really didn't let it bother me.

Finucan: We had a car fire one time on Eighteenth Avenue that I had five deaths in. The car drove into a store front. We thought that we had a store on fire because it looked like a store fully involved. We just figured it was another three story frame going with a store on the first floor. It was a corner building. I can remember somebody saying to me, "There's a car in there! There's a car in there!" It didn't register because it was a store and it was fully involved. There's a car in there? It didn't look like a garage to me and I'm wondering what the hell they're talking about. Then the civilians said, "Yes, there are people in there!" And sure enough we had five people in a car. Kids, I guess, they were joy riding or whatever and they all got killed. This was in the late '70s. There were five deaths in that fire, I remember that. My memory is not that good. I've been to many fires where we've had multiple deaths, four or five deaths.

Cosby: You feel frustrated when there's a fire death in your first due area. What you start doing is second-guessing yourself. Maybe you could have done this. Maybe you could have done that to save the people, especially if it involved children. There was a fire that happened later on in my career, which really stood out. This was a vehicle fire too. It happened on a Sunday morning. It was Bergen Street and Sussex. The way I was told it happened is these ladies were on their way to church. They had come off of Route 280 onto Bergen Street. They were headed for Sussex Avenue. An oil truck hit them. It was on a Sunday morning. It was right at the change of shifts.

We rushed to the scene. Seven Engine was first due. But when we got there, all we saw was the whole street was just one big smoke ball. The whole street was covered with black smoke. You really couldn't see anything. I was driving the apparatus. So what I did when I got to the smoke, I just pulled the rig to the side of the road. I didn't want to ride into the smoke because I didn't know what I was riding into. So, just pull it over to the side and then we stretched the inch and three-quarter hose into the smoke. When the smoke cleared, the only thing we could see were these three ladies sitting in the car. They were burned to death. They looked like manikins sitting in the car.

I kind of second guessed myself at that fire. I was thinking maybe if I had gone another way and came in on the other side, maybe we could have seen that. Because the only thing we could see was the black smoke. If we had come in on the Orange Street side, I just wondered could we have saved, maybe saved the people. Like I said, a lot of times you second guess yourself at a fire. I think it might have made some difference, but I don't know.

The eerie thing about this too was we thought everybody was dead in the car. We really couldn't approach the car right away because there was a power line lying on top of the car. As we were getting ready to approach the car, a hand came up from underneath the dashboard of the car. It was all charred and everything. We knew somebody was still in there alive, so we managed to get the power line off the car. We grabbed this lady out and they rushed her to the hospital, but she died. She didn't have a chance.

McDonnell: The building collapse with Ray Frost and myself will always stay in my mind. Ray Stoffers was right behind me. He made it back. The whole third floor was gone. I had been a Captain for two nights. It was our first day. We came in and went there. The first tour was already in the firehouse. I remember going up. It was on Sixth Street. We turned the corner and I saw the back. I was like "Oh, my God." The whole back of the building was burnt. There was no side wall. There was no roof, no wall. I said "Oh my God! That thing looks like it's going to collapse." We went in. We just had to overhaul. We had to go in. I really didn't want them to go in, but I was afraid to say "Wait. Let me take a look at this." That's what I wanted to do. I just wanted to go and look and decide for myself. But I was a new captain and these guys were all experienced, Kenny Miller, Ray Frost, Ray Stoffers, Ronnie Ricca. I didn't want to say anything.

Then we got up to the third floor. Mr. Macho, went banging away. It was nothing and I said, "Ray, come back from out there." It was stuff smoldering. Curtis Moore had a line just hitting it. As he was walking back, there was a crack and the floor buckled. He was right in front of me at that point. He started to fall. I reached for him and he just dropped right under my hand. He was gone. I remember looking and everything started going down like water goes down the sink. Everything started going, all these bricks. I remember I froze. I remember looking and saying, "My God. He's going to die." Ray Stoffers was right behind me. He stepped back off, like you would go into the next room. He just made it back onto that part. I froze, that's why I went because I froze. I looked and I realize the building was collapsing.

I started to go back and got two steps on the floor. I just saw the floor pull away from the wall. I just gave up. I said, "I'm going." All I tried to do was keep my balance. We went down. He went down. He got buried. I landed on top of it. I thought he was dead. I heard him yelling. He was yelling, "Help! Get me out!" That was the best sound I heard in my time on the job. I thought he was dead. I got up. I thought I was on the second floor. I didn't realize. He sounded like he was so far. I was standing in the basement actually on the pile of rubble and he sounded to me like he was down so far. I turned and saw the floor. I got up and went to get out of the building. I went running through the building. I ran out through the apartment and out the front door and I fell down the front stairs. I was screaming "We got to get Ray! We got to get Ray!"

They all came running down. Twelve Engine was there. We went around the back and we dug. After a while we found him. Ronnie had run to the truck and called for another alarm. He said there was a building collapse and guys were trapped. They were yelling like that. The guys who were going off on the first tour came back. These companies got there so fast. We had found Ray and were clearing his face. After the guys came, we dug him out and he was pretty messed up.

I hit my leg on something just before I landed, but I thought I was going to die. I remember when I landed; I felt my helmet bounce off. And then all the shit started hitting me in the head. I just put my hands on my head and I screamed because I was waiting for the rest of the building to come down on top of me. There was a chimney that was six foot wide. I went right down the side of it, next to the chimney.

* * * * *

Another time Al Fraser and I almost got killed. It was a miracle we got out alive. It was another fire with three or four buildings. This was an abandoned building that I went in. I was the only one in. I went in the building, went up to the third floor. There was fire in the building. I went to the back and saw there was fire in the back. I started to back out of the building. By the time I got back to where I started, it was completely black. I couldn't find my way out of the building. I finally found the doorway into the stairway. I went into the stairway and came down. Al Fraser was in the Tact Squad. He was coming up with a line. So I said, "Al, it's up in the cockloft." He said, "Okay." So we went in and he opened the line. The air started hissing out so I opened the ceiling.

I pulled the ceiling and said it's up in the cockloft. It's pitch black now you can't even see and all of the sudden he starts screaming, "I haven't got any water! I haven't got any water!" What the hell was he talking about? I turned and he hit me in the chest and spun me around. My helmet came off. I reached up for my helmet and my head went right into the fire. I said, "Oh, Christ!" I turned for the doorway and I could see the outline of the doorway on fire. I thought, "Oh, shit! It came up the stairs." In fact, I had told him just before he shouted that I was going to go to the front and get the windows in the front. He ran to the front. I thought the fire came up the stairs behind us.

I started to go to the front windows. I don't know why. For some reason I had my arms out. I hit these French doors and I closed the doors behind me. Went to the front windows and took the windows out. I figured the firemen would save us. We're okay. We're yelling out the window. They didn't even look at us. We were screaming for our lives. The place was roaring behind us and I lost all my faith in firemen. I always had it in my mind that if you ever got trapped, you get to the window, yell, and the fireman will save you. We were screaming. Nobody even looked at us. We were up there yelling for our lives. God, nobody even looked at us.

My mind was going. I never thought clearer. You know how people who are in combat, they say their mind worked clearly. I never thought clearer in my entire life. I thought of every way to get out of that building that you could in about fifteen seconds. I used to do that. I used to do little mental exercises where I would always think to myself, "Okay, if this happens you can't get down the stairs. What would you do now? Where would you go?" I went through, "Okay, I'll rip the wall open and get into the stairway." Then I thought the fire came up the stairs, so I can't do that. We could jump. This is the third floor. If we jump out this window, we're going to die. We can't go back the other way. I was going through every way to get out of that building. I knew I couldn't jump. I was going to jump if I had to jump, but I wasn't going to jump unless I had to. I don't know why, but I thought of the line. I went back and I found the line. He had pulled the line into the front room with us. I went back and I opened the doors and the fire had lifted up off the floor and was going across the ceiling. So I yell to him to come to the line. Get to the line. He came. He said, "I've got the line." I said, "Let's follow the line out of the building." We just got out into the stairway and a couple of guys from the tact squad were coming up. I told them, "We got burned. Al's coming. He's burned, too." They took him. I took myself down. They took Al.

What had happened was the supply line burst in the street, so everybody lost water. It just happened when he was opening the line, because you could hear the air hissing out. Al thought he had water. We were lucky. We made it out of there just in time. Because Dick Tiffany, he was the one to come up the stairs. He went back to get the line. He said when he got up to the top of the stairs he couldn't get the line. It was so hot. He had to uncouple the hose in the stairway, pull the line down, and leave. He said, "You guys got out of there. In thirty seconds you would have been dead."

Pianka: An alarm I'll never forget. Three alarm fire on Avon Avenue and we're in the basement. It wasn't even our fire. It was a first tour fire. We're there the next day sloshing around in water looking for a baby. We finally find the baby. It could have been a roasted chicken really. But we weren't going to quit. We just kept doing it until we found that baby. It took us well into the morning, hours after the fire. There are a number of instances like that I remember searching.

*   *   *   *   *

When the building collapsed on Ray Frost, we were in the kitchen having coffee and all the sudden somebody starts screaming over the radio. We knew the first tour had a fire only a couple of blocks up the street, up Sixteenth Avenue. There was something about a collapse. We jumped on the rig, ran down there and evidently they had still been overhauling and for some reason Ray Frost had been on the third floor. They walked to the back of the building, which had been burnt out pretty good. They stepped into this pantry or kitchen. Anyway that whole section gave way.

We came down. I remember going there. He's buried under there, but you could hear him because he's pretty excited. He's screaming and all that. We have to get him out of there, so we're trying to get this stuff off. I remember Kenny Miller, he was in Five Truck at the time. He says, "Ray calm down. Don't worry about it. Everything will be okay. If you're not, we'll take care of your wife, don't worry about it." That sort of shut him up for a few minutes. Because we knew he was okay. We could hear him and you just had to calm him down somehow. Hey, relax. We're with you.

Rotonda: First big fire I had, an old lady and a grand-daughter passed away. She was afraid. She was only on the second floor. She was afraid to drop the kid to a guy who was trying to get her to drop the kid on a car. He was standing on top of a car. She wouldn't. She went back into the fire and disappeared. That was it. That was a little tough. Some of them are tough.

I can remember one bad one on Broadway and Grafton Avenue. We pulled up. We threw ladders up. A woman and her husband were on the balcony with three kids. Second guessing, we screwed up because we should have just put that bucket into work. We used the ladders. We got two kids down and the third was like a fifteen year old boy and he climbed on the ladder. He was going to try and get down and he fell off the ladder. The smoke inhalation knocked him off. He fell. We got the kids. The mother, I can still see the gold teeth in her mouth as she's handing me the kids. Everything was going bad. The wind was bad. The water wouldn't reach up to where they were and we tried to get the mother and father. We got the bucket in, but couldn't get it positioned right. It was like three feet away from the balcony, so Augie, Captain Schultz, and I were in the bucket. I jumped from the bucket onto the balcony trying to get the mother and father who handed me these kids.

That's another thing I learned. In the movies, it's a lot of baloney. You don't pick up unconscious people. They weigh a ton and they're like soup. I couldn't move them. I'm hollering for them to pour the water right in. I figured to bring a little oxygen in at least. I'm trying to get this guy and he wasn't a big guy. I could hardly move him. I'm trying to get him with his head over the balcony, so maybe he can get some oxygen. Now I didn't know if they were still alive or not, to tell you the truth. They were out though. I couldn't budge them. The water, it reached the second floor, but with the wind, it wouldn't reach the third floor where I was. I wanted them to just pour water right on top of the whole deal here, couldn't reach it. The wind was bad. Everything was bad.

So Augie and Shultz were telling me, "Get the hell out of there." They're hollering for me to get out and my back is towards the doorway behind me. In the meantime the doorway blows out right over my back. I was bent over, so it really didn't get me. It got Augie and Captain Shultz. They burnt their ears. They were cursing, but they wouldn't leave me. They're hollering, "Will you get out of there? Will you get out?" They're cursing at me, but I was so upset over these two people and like I said I could still see that woman. She had the biggest smile like she was all right. And yet they weren't.

We lost three people that day, the mother, father, and somebody else downstairs. It's hard to handle for something like that and I'm still thinking of that woman with the gold teeth smiling while she's handing me the kids. And yet we lost her and the husband. So it was a hell of a tragedy that time. It really bothered me a lot. It still bothers me a lot.

* * * * *

We don't realize what we're doing to ourselves a lot of times, physically or mentally, whether it's sucking in all that smoke and everything else. To us it's like part of the job. You're going to do the job, whatever it takes to get it done. You don't realize how it's affecting you overall. What you do to your body today is going to show up tomorrow. I think that's where the firemen seem to end up with a little bit shorter life span. We don't know what we really did to ourselves until all of the sudden it's over. I don't know. You just hope for the best anyway. But it's true. We don't really know. All that smoke and shit like that, you don't know what you're doing to yourself because as healthy as you're going to be, as you get older nothing operates the same. You start finding out this is wrong and that's wrong. That'll scare the hell out of you, I guess.

T. Grehl: I don't think we ever second guessed ourselves. What we could have done. What we couldn't have done. The guys I worked with were phenomenal. They did whatever they could from beginning to the end. You might have second guessed yourself. Should I have gone in the left door instead of the right door when the person was on the right? You know that possibly, but I'd say every fire that we went to where a person died, there weren't that many where they weren't dead before we got there. So you couldn't really second guess yourself because it's just too involved. If these guys, not me, if these guys couldn't make it, it was too late anyway.

Ryan: Been in a couple of icky places, a couple of collapses, stuck in collapses. The one most vivid was the one I was right by the porch. I was able to get out by myself. The other I was stuck inside. I was in the first floor of the building and stuck in a void. The building came down, partial collapse of the building and of course you get all the crazy thoughts running through your head. And hot, fortunately I had the tip with me and I'm putting it all over me. I'm keeping me from being on fire. I think we were only one and two that night, so I was there by myself. First due, first floor came down, stuck in a void. I hollered and screamed. But I had water, so I was okay. I was only in there for a few minutes, but it's an experience you really don't want to be too repetitive.

It's getting hurt and hurt a lot of times. Everybody that does the job right is going to get hurt. It's just a fact of life, because you're going into unstable buildings where something destructive is happening. The floor's going to go, you're going to walk through a floor; you're going to fall in a hole. I fell in a hole and dislocated my elbow in a job up in the Burg. Twenty-six breaks in that. That was fun. Twenty-six breaks in my elbow. They stuck it all back together.

Another time I was driving Eleven Truck. A box came in for Fifteenth Avenue and Fifteenth Street. I guess it was about two o'clock in the morning, three o'clock in the morning. I'm not sure. It was early morning hours. There was some kind of difficulty with the radio communications. Six Engine was on the scene. The fire actually was on Sixteenth Avenue and Eighth Street. They had people in the window. It was a heavy back porch fire in a very large three story frame. Probably six family, possibly a nine family, it was a very big three story frame, right on the corner. Upon arrival I spotted the aerial. There was a man actually hanging outside of a window on the third floor and he was hollering that my children are inside. Tommy Reiss was beside me.

We raised the ladder up to get this one fellow. I went up to the window where the man was hanging out. As I got within about three feet of the window, the room and the whole top floor was engulfed in flames, blowing the windows out. Blew the fellow out, seared all the skin off his whole body. I was maybe three, four feet away from three children. They were in a bedroom. They were all looking at me when the fire actually engulfed them. And I saw them. The only thing I could think of is like flowers wilting right before me. I was very close. I was within three, four feet. I was burnt, pretty good. I had second degree burns on my entire left arm through my coat, left side of my face. Had to be eventually taken to the hospital after we knocked it done.

There's a woman hanging out of the third floor window. Nine Truck had thrown their ladder up underneath her and with the fire conditions, they encountered the same problem. They just were just too short, ten seconds, fifteen seconds too short. But I had eye contact with all three kids when that happened. I actually had to go talk to a priest that day because it really bothered me. Six Engine made a couple of good grabs off the front of the building raising ground ladders or off of other ground ladders thrown. And this was a case of arson.

There was some radio difficulty at that time and the repeater was off. So, the other companies were being dispatched to Fifteen Avenue and Fifteenth Street with the fire on Sixteen Avenue and Eighth Street. Six Engine swung around the corner going on Sixteenth Avenue and the fire was right there. They're hollering on the radio. No one could hear them. We were coming across Ninth Street, saw the glow there and Six Engine was in the front, while everybody else was going up a little higher, going across Twelfth Street. For some reason that evening, I went over Ninth Street. And that's the operations at that fire. There was just no chance to save anybody. I believe there were seven people killed at that fire.

Langenbach: Milford Avenue, I almost died in a fire. I'll never forget that. I was in Five Truck again and we caught a job. It was a three story frame. Fire was on the first and second floor and we didn't have our aerial ladder. The aerial was broken. I was tillering, get off and we see a guy walking in the third floor window with the fire behind him, so we threw a thirty-five foot. Go up there. I get up the ladder and I try to reach the guy. Now he flopped half way out the window. It was snowing. It was cold. Reach in and try to grab him and I can't move him. I'm getting pissed, so I finally jumped inside the room. I took my mask and put it on him and now I'm in trying to move him. Well, what it was when he flopped out the window his feet hooked under the radiator. So, I can't lift him out. I have to take his feet out. We finally get the guy out, get him down.

Cassidy comes up; they put another thirty-five foot ladder up. Cassidy comes up and he hands me a booster line because now the fire's in the room with me. Now all this time I didn't have the mask on, my mask. So, I'm standing there looking at the booster. I'm looking at the fire, looking at the booster. I'm say, "I know they go together, but I don't know what this is for. I know what that is and I'm pretty sure, but . . . ." I remember this like it was yesterday. Making that kind of like decision process. I know what this is. So, I finally said, "Screw this." I threw the thing down and went back down the ladder. Well, by the time I got to the bottom, I passed out. I stopped breathing there. Johnny Fagan threw me in the chief's gig, took me to Barnabus. I stopped breathing again and then I was there for a couple of days. Just burnt, I had burnt my throat, inside my lungs.

*　*　*　*　*

I was a captain in Six and I was the acting Battalion Chief. We had a fire right off of South Orange Avenue. We lost six people. I'll never forget that. It was just one of those things. It looked like ten cents worth of fire, by the time we got inside there were people stacked up all over the place, dead. Then you go back to the firehouse and you start second guessing yourself. Now I'm not thinking of it as a captain because I knew what a captain would have done. I'm thinking, "Well, I'm the Battalion Chief. Do I have to tell these guys? Did I do the right thing?" Tough, tough stuff.

Connell: We had several deaths at fires on High Street. Later on in your career you remember the deaths, but you can't put them with the fires any more for some reason or other. You learn to disassociate. I was pretty good at leaving anything I saw or happened on the job there. I didn't take it with me. I could go home and forget about what happened. It wouldn't come back to my mind again until I came back to work the next day. When I was home I never carried my baggage home with me. It's just something in my psyche. A death might affect me at a fire, but once I'm off I'm okay until I get back to the firehouse. Then I'll start thinking about it again. While I'm at work, I'll think about it. When I'm off work, I disassociate it.

Once I found out there is a death or I come across one, I tried to figure how long the person has been dead. Did he die after we got there or was he dead before we got there? During Incident Safety Officer Class they brought something up that I never really thought about before when you're going in for a search and everything else. Are you going in for a rescue or are you going in for a recovery. I never thought about it in those terms until I had the Safety Officer course. But basically, that's what I was doing before. I was trying to figure out, was there something as a truck man I could have done? Could I have saved this person? Could I have gotten in there? Is he dead because I screwed up or somebody in my company screwed up? Was he gone before we got there? I think any fireman will tell you this. Any fire you go to where there is a death, you wonder is there something you did or something that could have been done differently that could have prevented it? It's a slap in the face to you. You don't come on this job to be in the recovery business. You come on this job basically to be in the rescue business. If you have the recovery frame of mind, you're probably not going to be a truck man. You're probably not even going to be a fireman or remain on this job.

Pignato: My first real fire had to be on Dickerson and Third. It was a two and a half story frame. We put the aerial ladder up to the top window to ventilate the window. There were supposed to be kids trapped in there. I threw my tank on and climbed up there. I got my hook stuck in the blinds while I was taking out the window and I couldn't get it out. I'm trying to get my hook unstuck and all of the sudden the blinds sucked in, which is classic sign of a backdraft. There's an explosion or a poof. I look in the alleyway to my right. The flames blew the windows out the side of the house from where I was. Jumped six foot across the alley way and started the next house on fire.

The fire came out from underneath me. I'm trying to get down this ladder. I get hooked on a wire, probably a telephone wire. Otherwise I would have fried by now. I'm stuck on this wire and my tank gets stuck. I'm trying to get out of this wire. The fire is starting to come up by the ladder. I final got myself out and I climb down.

I see all these guys from Eleven Engine lying on the side walk. They're burnt or hurt. What happened was as I was popping the windows up there. All the guys were trying to get in the front door. They busted in the front door. It was so hot the lock was melted. They got in there. Back then they had the Macks and they only had a three hundred gallon tank. Seven Engine was the second due engine. Fifteen had to come from the other side. Meanwhile the engine driver is trying to hook up to the hydrant. He hooks up to the hydrant, but the little pentagon on top was gone. Somebody had sawed the brass thing off there. I remember him banging on the hydrant with a maul, a sledge hammer. He's trying to crack the bonnet. If he cracked the bonnet, he can open it up with a Stillson Wrench. The next hydrant was all the way off out on Central Avenue. It was just so far away.

They had gone in there as far as they could with six hundred gallons. They ran out of water. The air they had introduced into this building, now fed the fire. Now they had no water. It blew back at them. That's when it blew out the side windows and started to burn them. They came tumbling back out. To add a little spice to this, there were two boys in there yelling for help. They died in the fire. They didn't die from the smoke condition. They were cooked, burned alive. I heard some noises, but at the time I didn't know what it was.

It was rather new to me, seeing the guys get burnt. I never saw firemen burnt before. I got little burns myself as a volunteer, but nothing like this. One guy's hand was burnt up. Other guys were trying to make it into the building. They got a supply. Somebody was back-stretching all the way back to Central Avenue, a couple of blocks, because they couldn't find a hydrant in that area. The kids were left home alone. That was one of the many fires I've been to where they leave the kids home alone. That was my first fire.

* * * * *

The only other fire we had that was memorable to me was a three story frame, six family. I think it was one of the first fires I am acting captain. We're oh and three. Get in front of the building. We got two guys to go to the roof. I was going inside the building. We're first due. The engine's hooking up. They're busy doing whatever they're doing. I see there are no companies in there. It's two or three o'clock in the morning, there have to be people in the building. There aren't that many outside the building. So I went in there.

I went up the stairs and I got to the hall where the two apartments divide off and the doors were open. It was real hot. I got down and I tried to crawl into one of the apartments until my ears started to burn and I had to back out of there. It was just too hot. I wasn't going to go too far in by myself. Just then a guy passes me on the stairs. Comes up on the stairs and there was a staircase going up to the roof, a regular stairs, not a ladder. He takes a couple of steps and he starts opening up the cockloft. I was studying at the time and I said, "Never ever open it up from inside the building." So I tried to stop him. I heard the sky light break as I was going up the stairs, but I never heard the K-12 saw, I never heard any chopping upstairs. And they never opened the door up at the top of the penthouse.

Well what happened was the roof collapsed in the back. Blew the fire out of the hole the guy made. He was burnt right through his coat. He was in the hospital for a long time. I was burned up my arms, all the hair on my head was gone, and my neck was all burnt. I had the new 880 polycarbonate helmet and it had an air space all around it. I used to use the leather helmet I had from Long Branch, but they said no. Now I had to wear this helmet. So I got this helmet on. The only way I keep it on my head; I had to keep the chin strap on me. The fire went inside this and burnt the whole top of my head. It was like you put your face inside a flame thrower.

I jumped over the banister. Figured I have to get out of here. I'd never been burned like that before. Down I go. I tumble down the stairs and I landed on the next landing and my helmet stayed on my head. Then I jumped down the next landing because the fire is still all around me. It turned out the fire went down the three stories. It came out into the street, the blast. It burnt twelve other guys just coming up the stairs.

I finally get all the way down the stairs. The other guys are mostly banged up because they lost their helmets in the mad rush to get out of the building. Mine was still on. My face mask was pulled up over my eyes. I thought I was blind, that my eyes were burnt. That's what I'm worried about more than anything else. I'm yelling out in the street, "I can't see." Finally, I pulled my mask off, I could see. But my skin was all coming off. They put us in the back of the rescue truck. So we're in the back of the truck.

Now, all the other guys are in the truck. I'm looking at their boots. Everybody had a band that went around their boot. This guy had a stripe going down. At that time you could buy whatever kind of boots you wanted and his strip went down. Nobody had those boots on. And I kept saying, "There's somebody missing! There's somebody missing! I'm telling you.

There's somebody missing!" And they wouldn't pay any attention to me. Until we get half way there, the captain of the Rescue Squad who was also burned says, "They took somebody, I just found they took somebody in the Chief's gig to another hospital." That was that guy.

*   *   *   *   *

Another night, it had been uneventful before this alarm, just a lot of false alarms. We should have been the third due truck on the box, but we're the first due truck because companies are out. Six Engine was first due. We get up there. Six Engine is in front of the building. They're pulling off hose. This house is all by itself. There's a one story garage on one side of it. I look at the building, there's fire showing in every window. Your typical vacant building well torched. Now we're trying to go to the roof, but we just can't get to it. There're flames coming out of every window. The guys made an effort to make the front door. They really weren't going to do much with an inch and a half hose. So, the Chief ordered us, Truck Eleven, to take a two and a half up to the garage roof. Surround and drown. Up we go, throw a ladder up. We climb up there, make a little circle with the hose and start to put water on this thing. Probably about a half an hour later, if that, Chief DeTroia comes up with a look on his face. I said, "Chief, what's the matter?" He was a Captain at Eleven Truck for a while, before he got promoted. So, I got to know him a little bit. I said, "What's the matter, Chief?" He says, "I think I have seventeen people in this building."

Just then the wind changed direction and blew the smoke in our faces. I said, "This is an abandoned building isn't it?" We all thought it was an abandoned building. "No, there're seventeen people missing." Well the seventeen turned out to be twelve. We did have twelve people dead in that building. But, they were dead probably, even before we left the firehouse. That was a fire that made the paper. But the building was fully involved.

You didn't know it was occupied. I wish I hadn't known it was occupied until I went home because you knowing people are roasting inside there. That's a bad feeling. You can't do anything for them. That's a pretty bad feeling.

*   *   *   *   *

When I was at Rescue we had a box come in for Down Neck. They had a working fire, five or six victims inside the building, never said anything. We hop in the rig. We shoot on down there. They're already pulling people out. They were pushing this eighteen or nineteen year old boy out the window. I ran over to the EMS to get a gurney. I put a burn sheet on it. I put him on this burn sheet. He was burned from the waist up. The rest of him was fine. So, I checked the airway to make sure his throat wasn't burnt. I figured he had a shot at living. He's jumping all around. He's still conscience. We tried to get him into the ambulance. We get him into the ambulance. We work on this guy to keep him alive, tried to revive him and keep him alive. Put an airway in if he goes out. Just then Apostolico jumps in and he's got an eighteen month old baby. It's in diapers. Hands me the baby. I take the baby. The baby's fine from the diaper down. It was only burned from the waist up. It looked like a real doll. Its skin was so hard from being burned, but the rest of the baby was limp. I looked down the baby's throat and it was burnt all the way down. It's dead. There's no way you're going to save this baby.

Langevin: As a rule you don't question yourself if there's a death at a fire you're at. After a couple of fires we had, I would say to myself, "Is there something I could have done more to maybe save this person's life? Could I have gotten the ladder up quicker? Could I have done this? Could I have done that?" It doesn't haunt me.

Perdon: I had the fire where we lost twelve people. I was at that one. I was at Seventeen Engine still when we had that one though. We were third due. Six Engine was first due.

Jimmy Edgar was trying to make his way in there on the stairs, but it was like top to bottom, completely involved. You just couldn't do it and then they went to outside water. At another one we lost five kids. That's where I found the little baby girl on the third floor. That's where all five of the kids were up there, but there was a fire on the first floor. Eighteen was there. I had to try and make it up to the third floor, but there was this fire on the first floor. This was when Lalor was roving. He had just become a captain. So, he was saying, "You got to come back down. You got to come back down. We got fire on the first floor." So, I'm trying to move with the line, just to get it turned because the stairs were so hot. When I tried to make a move without any the line opened you could hear like sssss. You could hear it, actually hear it. With that though they just pulled the line right from my hand, but I managed to wet it a little bit, the whole stairs. So, I'm figuring, "Well, let me give it one more shot without a line." With that Tony Miedler breaks the window behind me and the whole thing was so hot the fire just blew down the stairs. You could hear it. It sounded like a train coming at me.

I just laid flat back. It went over me. Eighteen Engine was just getting ready to go into the second floor apartment. It got them, burnt the shit out of them. It went down as far as the middle of the first floor staircase and caught the captain of Nine Truck on the first floor staircase going up, burnt his ears. They found him walking down the block. He was in shock. But as soon as it blew over, I went back and I got up. Went back to the third floor and I found the baby underneath the rug. Right there at the top of the landing, but inside the door. The reason I'm giving you that description is because Chief Melody was interviewed by one of the prime channels about how we couldn't find the baby. They said the baby was found on the stairs, in the middle of the stairs.

He had the reporter go to the Academy. They made smoke in the tower there and they put a baby doll there. And the reporter missed the doll on the stairs, so she could understand. But I told Chief Melody, I said, "Wait a minute. I found that baby, but it wasn't on the stairs. That baby was underneath a rug or a big towel and just inside the door on the third floor." And the sister, who I found, she was like a little bit behind her, must have put the baby there for extra protection because she never made it. She collapsed. She was already rigor mortis. I remember taking her down. She reminded me of one of those Patty Play-pal dolls, three foot dolls. I just took her down to the second floor. I didn't bring her outside. I brought the baby outside because I thought it was still good, but the sister I just brought to the second floor and didn't want to bring her out, rigor mortis had set in. I don't know how the story got out that the baby was found on the middle of the stairs and how we couldn't find her.

*   *   *   *   *

You do feel a sense of defeat when there's a death at a fire, all the time. I'm my worst enemy though. I'm highly critical of myself. I'll beat myself up. I'm truthful. If I feel I didn't push hard enough, I'll be the first one to admit it. One time Vinnie Kuhn wound up getting the kid out, but he went up through the outside on a ladder and I tried the interior. The place was just blazing too much, but I had a good shot. I thought I should have made it. And that one beat me up. I felt bad on that one; it was like I should have made it. But the fire was converging from two doors and I had to make that turn through it. I felt I should have and could have. You know what, as I came out it blew out with me. And Joe McCarthy closed a door on me. He didn't realize I was in there. So, now I had to come back, find a door, and I snuck out a hallway door. I felt bad on that, but other than that, no. It doesn't work. I'm just by nature, I'll be the first to tell you I screwed up or I didn't try hard enough.

Bisogna: A few times I got nervous to the point of, "What am I doing here? I don't need this job." One was a situation in a third floor apartment that several kids died in. That was the worst and I had just had a baby who was a couple years old. Richie Bennett had a baby and you're pulling kids out of these cribs who are dead. That was the worst.. I walked out of there saying, "Forget this job. I can't stand this." But you get over that. My daughter asked me the other day, "Have I ever smelt flesh?" And I told her, "Yes, a couple of times." If you're an adult, you screwed up. But the babies, that's the one that hurts, especially not just one. It was three or four kids, went from infant to probably six or seven. That affected me at the time. Especially, I had my own little daughter too. Maybe if I was still a young kid who didn't care about anything. That was probably my worst day. But there haven't been too many of those thank God.

Ricca: We had a fire on Nineteenth Street. I was on the job a few months. George Caswell impressed upon me, when you're searching, if it feels like a person, make sure it's not a dog and you go yelling crazy. I think it was Nineteenth Street, I crawled into this one room. There was a family. The father was on top of the mother and the mother was on top of the baby. All three of them died, but they each protected each other. And the first thing I felt was dog, I thought, to my left. Later on I felt the bodies, I felt the arms. It was my first time, I started screaming. The first thing when the guys came in is they went to the dog. And I heard somebody say, "Hey, J O, it's the dog." Then they realize the people were next to them. The dog had died first.

*   *   *   *   *

Right before we were laid off we were interviewed by Eyewitness News or Channel Four, one of them. They left and about an hour after they left, a guy on Fifteenth Street up from the firehouse died smoking in bed. It was the actual first time I went in and really saw someone because the other people were at night and it was dark. This guy was in the daylight and I saw him. I was frightened. I started thinking twice about the job at that point. That came shortly after the other people that I was upset about. Here is this guy. I pictured the poor guy, a hard day at work, lying down in bed taking a smoke and now he's dead. One room bedroom fire, the typical go in, coining the phrase "splash, splash, splish, splish." We were done. The smoke cleared and there's a guy in the bed. Four deaths within a few months, that stayed with me a long time, to today.

*   *   *   *   *

The bad times, Ray Frost got buried twice. That's probably the worst thing I remember. I was always mad at Chief O'Donnell for that, Dinky O'Donnell. We were brought up to this house, Tommy's a new captain, Finucan's fairly new. Tommy didn't like the look of the building, didn't want to say anything because I guess he was new. I think he held back a little. We went up. Kenny Miller was on the second floor. Ray Stoffers, Ray Frost, and Tommy were going out into the rear of the building. Tommy turns to me and says, "Don't you come here." I was always a big guy. He says, "Don't you come in here." With that there was a crack and I saw Tommy in mid-air like he was diving off a diving board and your brother holding onto a two by four. I just bee lined to the radio and I just started saying "Emergency" in it. I told them we had a building collapse. After my transmission Finucan came over the walkie-talkie. They said, "Twelve Engine, we got that already."

I turned and looked after I ran to help them dig. There was the United States Marine Corps, Joe Lefchak, Myles McDonald, and Brian Ewing. There were guys coming out of the wood work, coming to help, but making matters worse because they were stepping on him. Tommy was smart enough to get off him. We found his hands in his gloves and you would think you dig one way you'd find his head, one way you'd find his feet. It didn't work that way. For some reason, the way he was rolled up, his head was nowhere near his gloves. I remember, Joe Lefchak put a helmet on his head because shit was falling as he was working. And Joe was in there, one of the first guys, up to his elbows digging. We pulled him out and me and Ray Stoffers drove the rig home. I remember we fronted the rig right in. Then Tommy sent us to get Ray's wife Angie.

This happened like first thing on a Sunday morning because I was coming from the shore. And I'm driving down with Ray. I think we had Ray Frost's car. It was a '65 Chevy we were driving. I said, "Ray, what do we tell her?" We were both, "I don't know. What do we tell her?" So, I told her that he was in a building collapse and we think he broke his arm.

He's got to sign something, but he's stubborn and wouldn't sign. They wanted to drill a hole in his stomach the size of a dime to check for internal injuries. My brother Joe was working the first tour at that time, he came up and he's talking with Ray. "Ray let them do what they got to do." Everybody was trying to help out. Tommy was on a spine board in the hospital where he was worrying about Frost and that was it. He didn't know. He was up and down, jumping up and down.

The look on Angie's face, I remember that. Bring her back. What made me feel good was when we sold tickets for a basket of cheer and everybody was real generous. We raised like twenty-five hundred dollars for him. I played Santa Claus. We went down to his house; brought presents for Christmas. Everybody really did care.

But the albatross is named Ray Frost. We had a building on Springfield Avenue. After he ended up coming back, we had a building on Springfield Avenue and there's a baby lost in it. It was a total burn out. They're steam shoveling chucks of the building and we had to search. I'm standing on a hill of dirt with Ray Frost and the bucket goes out of control and starts swinging over us. So I flatten down as much as I could. Ray jumps; goes over the fence and his pants get caught on the fence. Now he's hanging there. The bucket's swinging over me and him. Tommy's screaming. I'll never forget the looks on Tommy's face when something bad would happen. After the guy got control of the boom he says, "You get away from him and don't go near him ever again." Ray Frost got the albatross.

* * * * *

We come in the one day and Richie Bennett was working there at this time. We rode in together. The Tact Squad was in the yard and it was five-thirty. I said, "Richie, something happened. I got a feeling something happened." It was the day Ray fell from the ladder and the same thing. Go get the car. Go down and get Angie. "Richie, Ronnie what happened? Tell me." So we told her he was busted up bad. She took a lot. She's a good woman.

* * * * *

There is a price firemen pay for their job in terms of emotional baggage. The longer I'm on the more emotional I get. Just recently I'm coming off of two bad experiences and one good experience. People don't realize it. I don't even know if your family realizes it. But to hold a baby in your arms dead and to know that you have a baby her age at home, that happened to me on another occasion. That was later on in my career, but I still pictured my daughter's face when I flipped the kid over, with the little pajamas and the feet in it. No, it does. It's very, very emotional and it's so emotional that a guy like Joe Lefchak, who hid them pretty good, it even affected him. The roughest, toughest, it does.

I think there should be more help for guys. The first thing that happens when you have a fire death, the jokes start happening or the tension breakers, the stress relievers, that somebody will say something to try to break the tension, but they are the guys who are getting affected the worse. So, there really should be some type of counseling because nobody's going to ask for it.

*   *   *   *   *

I've been hurt once pretty seriously and never saw anyone from the city or never got a note from the city. We had a fire on Milford Avenue and Anthony Vanarelli was working for Joe Bisogna. Vanarelli had just passed his probationary time. Milford Avenue, three story connected, a frame, we go in to search the first floor because, of course, someone out on the street said the baby was in there which was normal, "My baby's inside" routine. There was a convertible, a sleeper sofa. When I searched a bed I used to like to lay on it and do a reverse angle wing. I started stepping up on the bed and there's an explosion in the basement. A fire ball came rolling up over our heads. Anthony, being new, I went to grab just to get him low. He kicked me in the head as he jumped off the couch and went out the first floor window. I lost my helmet and I started groping for my helmet. The ceiling collapsed and laid me out. I saw the ray of light under the door because I had reversed myself. I said to myself, "That's the way out." So, I dragged myself out. Brian Dardis grabbed me and started pulling me through.

Captain McDonnell, who had been in the first floor when the fire ball erupted, jumped out onto the porch. I told him, "Tommy" I said, "Cap, there's guys in the basement." We didn't know who they were at the time.

An engine company was maintaining an exterior line on the building. I went over and I said, "We need the line. We've got guys in the basement." And I ripped the line out of the captain's hands. I've seen Tommy do many things, but Tommy put that line on wide angle fog, pushed that fire back. I went in behind him. I opened the basement door and out came Richie McLaughlin, who was fairly new, had about the same time as Vanarelli. With that Joe Lardiere was at the top of the steps. He says, "I can't move, give me a hand." So, I helped pull him up to the top of the landing. I said, "Joe, I'm spent. You've got to help me." He said, "I can't." Tommy stayed, with the fire just lapping out the doorway, on wide angle fog and he's saying, "Ronnie, get him out of here." We dragged him outside. Then with the help of Brian and I think somebody from Nineteen Engine, they started working on him. But then I realized my back was really, really hurting. I was starting to tighten up.

That's when the whole thing started with my back. As a matter of fact, they had brought me to the hospital and Tommy was insistent that I get checked because when I went in the second time with him we had our masks off. So, the doctor at University wanted to keep me overnight and I'm fighting with him. He said, "We're going to have to inspect your throat." I have a rather large proboscis. He pulled out this thing, looked like a garden hose, he was going to stick down my nose. Well, he checked my throat and for some reason or other, they were going to keep me.

My brother Joe found out about it and takes my wife down to the hospital, which was probably the worst thing I ever want for her to see in my life. Kossup was at the fire and all I ever was asked was, "Are you all right?" That was the first and last time anybody ever called or checked or even stopped by in the hospital. I think I was kept for a night or two.

Gesualdo: We had a job on our second night. They had banged the second alarm immediately. We got there. There wasn't much water on the fire. It was fire just blowing out every window. To me it was just like wow. This shit burns. Nothing like you would ever have thought. In England we never saw anything like that because everything was brick and stone. To see this structure just totally engulfed and the thing that stuck in my head at that point was that I remember twelve people died in that fire and I believe eight of them were children, four adults.

Three days later coming back on our day shift, you think you'd block it out of your head and all that, boom here it comes back again. We had to go back to the scene because they were still sifting through the debris for body parts and bodies. It was like ten o'clock in the morning. We went over there. I believe it was a truck company and an engine company there. And we were going through the debris with brooms and rakes and things. I remember finding parts of torsos and a foot at one time, a foot from a child. The Arson Squad was there. I remember Bob Radecke and I guess Nardone were there. They were bagging and tagging parts as we uncovered them. That's when it really sunk in that twelve people died in this structure.

I was kind of upset. After being in the service the death part didn't bother me as much. It seemed like they must have run out of bags or containers, but I remember when we found part of a child's foot and we were sifting it out. We had it in a shovel. I remember them putting it in a Dunkin Donuts box and that stuck in my head for the last twenty-five years. It's just one of those things that you think to yourself, "Man, this city isn't prepared for things like this. They have to rely on Dunkin Donuts boxes?"

It's just one of those things that stuck in my head. It just seemed disrespectful, I guess, at the time. I was like, "Do I want to do this for another twenty-four years?"

Chapter Five: Four Fours - Brothers Lost

Fredette: I remember when we had the accident at Kinney and Belmont Avenue, when Frank Corbett from Six Engine died. Six Engine and Five Truck hit. You see, they were taking the car tracks up on Springfield Avenue with the Belgium blocks. Between Morris Avenue and Belmont Avenue, they had that all ripped open. So when we had anything down there we had to go down Kinney Street to Belmont Avenue, then cut back to the north, towards South Orange Avenue, then go down South Orange Avenue. Five Truck wasn't looking for us. They were coming way over on one side of Belmont Avenue and we came out then we hit. That little metal step where the tillerman gets on went right through Corbett's kidneys. He lived a couple of days in City Hospital then he died. He was an old timer getting ready to get out. He was working on his helmet, wanted to give it to somebody else. He was scraping the old paint off with a piece of glass. Getting it all primed, to hand it over to a new fireman. He had maybe two weeks to go.

Kinnear: A firefighter's death was tragic. The first deaths that I recall of firefighters were the accident that Twenty Engine had on South Orange Avenue and Prince. We were responding to the same alarm, to Thirteenth Avenue and Boston. I guess it was two, three o'clock in the morning, between two and three. Twenty came out Prince Street. The engine was hit by a car that was going down South Orange Avenue; speeding down South Orange Avenue. It was hit about amidships right by the pump and two of the firemen died. Bill Manger and Ben Witkus were their names. I think those were the first deaths at a fire I saw. It was terrible. It was shocking. You never think those things are going to happen.

Like I said, we were going to the same box. When we got down around Belmont Avenue, you could see smoke and flames. We thought "Okay, we've got a working fire." A good job, you know. When we got to South Orange Avenue and Jones Street, we saw it down South Orange Avenue, all the smoke and flames. We thought it's a block or two away from where the box was pulled, but we figured "It's a fire. Let's go." We went down there and the one guy was still in the cab. He was burned. The other guy had gone down Boston Street and he was sitting on a porch. He was badly burned. He died a couple of days later. That was the first tragedy I remember involving firemen.

May 7, 1972 Pennington Street

Schoemer: It was a regular night. It was early when it happened. The bell hit. We were second due at it. One Truck's first due and we're second due. We responded. It was fully involved, a two and a half story frame. There was a store on the first floor and apartments on the second and third. It was abandoned; beat up pretty bad, so we knocked it down with big lines. Then we went in. My brother took an inch and a half off of Ten Engine and the two of us hooked up on Ten Engine. I took the hook and gave him a hand with the hose line. We went in. We were standing inside. A chimney had fallen down. We were standing on top of these red bricks, so we could get like half a floor up and shoot the line at the second floor. Then Freddy Mitchell came in.

My brother had the hose line. He was standing higher than me on the pile of bricks. Freddy got between us. I'm standing there and all I heard was *whack* and I was buried. They said it moaned and groaned. I never heard it. All I heard was *crack* and it was like getting hit with a railroad train. Boom, I went down and it was like unsettled. It felt like that. Now I know I've got fire on top of me. I'm in the fire. I could grab Freddy's coat. I grabbed it and shook him. I said, "Freddy, are you all right?" "I'm hurt," he says, "but I'm all right. I am." I said, "Where's my brother?" He said, "He's next to me." I said, "Is he moving? Is he doing anything? Can he talk or anything?" And I kept calling, "Bud, Bud." and he never answered.

Freddy's passing out. I couldn't get any response out of my brother. After a bit, because you lose track of time, you start hearing the saws. Looking through it, after the smoke cleared a little bit, I could see a port-a-lite, but I couldn't see anybody. They're sawing away, sawing away. They got my brother out first. They took him away to the hospital. Then they got Freddy out.

The saw was right by my ear. I said, "The guys from the Squad will saw my head off." Mike from the Squad stuck his head down. I said, "Your ugly mug is the best thing I've ever seen in my life."

From the time the building collapsed, which they banged in the third alarm right away, to the time I got to the hospital, which was midnight, I was in the fire two hours. I couldn't move. I had lost circulation. Lying there, my one arm was out, my helmet was knocked off and all bent. Good thing I had a muzzle on or I'd still be there. My arm was over my hook. My hook went right underneath me somehow. I could see this light in there and I could see my arm dangling and the hook. I couldn't move. I said, "Come on you jaded superman, you can move." I couldn't move anything. The most I could do was grab Freddy's coat, the most I could do. Then they got me on the stretcher and they rushed me over to the ambulance. A Captain from Ten Truck was riding in the ambulance with me and I said to him, "Could you check my back. I feel like I've got a nail stuck in my back." Right in the middle of my back, I was burned right next to the backbone. They had to carve it all out and then put skin grafts on. It was deep at the time, before all the fat tissue grew back and everything. But it felt like a frigging nail in my back from the burns.

Well, I'm burnt from my shoulder down to below my waist. Spot burns, but actually not flame burns, baking burns. Nothing ever happened to my gloves; nothing ever happened to my boots, the top of my boots is where the burns stop. I got a one inch strip where I had my one inch black belt for my pants. My coat was never burnt. They cut it off of me. I regret that I didn't have a liner on. I should have had a liner, but it was a humid, warm night. It was May, but it was warm. I don't like a lot of heavy clothes to start with. They cut my pants off. My pants never burned, my shirt never burned. They cut my clothes off me.

When it happened Sammy D'Midio came over from Three Truck. We got to be pretty tight. I saw him. I said, "Sammy, do me a favor. Go and check and see how my brother is. I know they got him out. I'm gonna be fine. I'm hurt bad. I understand that, but I'm gonna be fine. But go and check and see how my brother is." He said, "Okay, I'll get back to you." He never came back, because now my brother was dead. A couple of other guys came. I said, "Tell me how my brother is. I've been asking. I'm trying to find out." None of them would come back. Maybe they respected me. I don't know.

In the morning, I don't know, six o'clock or so in the morning, my wife, my father, and my mother came down to the hospital and my father told me "Your brother is dead." I said, "I figured as much because no one would get back to me."

Calvetti: My boys got killed down there on Pennington and Orchard. It was May of '72. I'm not sure of the date, sometime in May of '72. It was a night time fire. I forget what time it was. I'm pretty sure it was night though. Anyway, the box comes in. We're third due on the first alarm. I think that's what we are, second or third due on the first alarm.

My captain is Joe Agolia. We rode two pieces back then. So we went down McCarter Highway, made the right onto Pennington Street. We stretch in from the corner. Now the back of the building is going, the whole back is all involved. We took a big line off. We're knocking the fire down. We let Mike Melanco take the line. Mike Melanco and this other guy took the two and a half inch line. They put a stick on it and they're holding it out there. We went with inch and a half on top of a one story roof to the back of this building. We were going to go in on the second floor. I'm in the front. Joe Agolia is behind me. I get right to the window and I look at this building again. "Ah, this building ain't worth it." I back up. I'm not backed up more than ten, fifteen seconds, this joint comes down. Agolia says to me, "What the hell made you stop? I'm so happy you stopped." I said, "I don't know something told me not to go into this building."

But I didn't think anybody was in it because we were at the back of the building. We weren't in the front. We didn't know what was going on in the front. Now we're on the roof staring at this big pile of lumber. That's all it was, a big pile of sticks. Next thing I know, they're calling the captain off. He tells me to stay up on the roof and squirt water. He's gone. I found out later on that there's guys trapped in the building. They don't know they're dead right away. It turns out three guys died. Two captains and a fireman died. Captain LaTorre from Twelve Engine, Russell Schoemer from Five Truck, and Captain Lardiere from Four Truck.

Funny things, quirky things happen. Tommy Grehl doesn't have a hook. Imagine that, a fireman without a hook at a fire. He goes back for a hook, saves his life because he's out of the building. And there's no fire in the front part of the building or else they'd all be dead. Some of them went in there with no masks on their face at all and they're on the first floor when this thing came down. They were alive for a while before they died because Richie Schoemer was trapped with his brother. Russell died, Richie lived. Richie got a big hole in his back from where he got burnt. Freddie Mitchell was screwed up from being burnt and trapped. That was a sad day, I'll tell you what.

Like I said there was no fire in the front of the building because some of those guys went in without a mask. All the fire was in the back. I guess the front looked pretty good because we knocked it all down from the back with a big line. But something told me not to go into that jerk off building. What told me? I don't know. Who the hell knows? Luck.

Dougherty: We responded on the second alarm. In fact we went there. We went up a ladder to the second floor, Captain Hettinger went up to look around. He just peered in the window. We only had one piece at that time. The International was broken down. Pete Sheridan had moved over for Artie Conners who had passed away. He had just come from a truck company. It was me, Robshaw, Jimmy Donlon, and Pete Sheridan. When it happened, Jimmy was driving. Hettinger told Pete to take a two and a half off and we were told to take two rolled lines of inch and a half in.

Instead of pulling several lengths of two and a half off and letting Jimmy take the hydrant; Pete took one length of two and a half off. Jimmy went to take the hydrant, but there was only one length there. We had the two rolled lines on the sidewalk and Hettinger was on the ladder. He came down off the ladder screaming and yelling. "Hold it. What are you doing?" and the building collapsed. So, we were fortunate that Pete screwed up and we weren't in the building. Otherwise we would have been up there. All of this happened in just a matter of two, three minutes. We had to get away from there and it came down.

Well, there was a lot of screaming, yelling and it was very chaotic. I remember hearing screaming. There was a void on the side of the building. I went into the void and Bobby Jorda was in there and then Cliff Dainty was trapped in there. I remember telling them pass a line in because there was still some fire in the back and just wetting it because I knew the building had collapsed. So, I wet it down just a little bit, didn't go crazy with the water because you didn't know just where people were. Just to keep the fire away. Then Bobby Jorda was overcome because we couldn't lift the roof or push anything out of the way, there were two, three people trapped. There was Cliff Dainty and Lardiere, Captain Lardiere. So Bobby Jorda went out. Then Cliff was screaming his leg was burning, so I put a little water down his boot. Then I noticed Lardiere was folded over. The beam broke right on his back, folded him right over. All I could see was the back of his back. Actually, he was pinned right next to Cliff. That probably saved Cliff's life.

It happened so fast, it never even entered my mind at that time of what am I doing here or what the hell is this shit. It didn't. It's "What can I do to help somebody?" And then you're saddened. Like everything else, it's just a tragedy because later it sets in that these men had families.

I was only on the job two years, so I knew them for that amount of time. Cliff came on the job with me, so I knew him very well. I just looked at the people who survived that fire and who never lost their enthusiasm for the job. They were trapped in there, Cliff Dainty, Freddy Mitchell. They had men die right next to them. They lost Russell Schoemer. I just took my lead from those people.

T. Grehl: I lost my Captain on May 7, '72, Captain Lardiere, up on Orchard Street. We pulled up. Second alarm again, it was just a block or two the other side of McCarter Highway, in fact we parked on McCarter Highway. It was a very, very foggy night, rainy night. All the smoke was lying down and the Chief told us to stand by, that was over the radio. So, Lardiere decided to walk up to the fire and see what was going on. I was twenty-two, twenty-three at the time, just wanted to do anything. I had a hook. I started walking up behind him. He told me, "Stay here." I said, "Na, I'll walk up with you, see what you're going to do." Well, we got there. We walked around the corner and like I said you couldn't see a lot because the smoke was hanging down. We started to walk in the building and somebody yelled for a hook. "I got it." He says, "No, no, no, I got it. You go get a hook." "No, no, no get inside. I got it. Let me do something. I've been waiting for a fire forever. Let me do something." "No," he says, "I got it. Go get another hook off of Five Truck." I walked down. Five Truck was right there; I walked down and I couldn't reach the hook from the side I was on. So, I walked around the truck because it was on the other side of the truck, grabbed the hook, walked back in front of the building, the building collapsed, and he died along with Schoemer and LaTorre at that fire.

When the building collapsed everyone went crazy, because it just came down. We all knew the guys inside were buried. Everybody just started digging, looking for people. Schoemer's brother was buried also and he got out. He had burns on the back. Pretty deep burns if I remember on the back. They had sent us down there immediately. We were there.

The Battalion Chief sent us right back to quarters because they had apparently seen where Lardiere was and saw the collapse. He was killed instantly. His back was shattered. It had come down like that. So, just get out of here because we know you guys are screwed up mentally. Just go back to quarters. Just stay there. Get out of here. I'll tell you what. It was early evening because we got back to the firehouse before nine o'clock. We played cards and every single night exactly at nine o'clock Lardiere's wife would call, exactly. And he would leave the card game and go answer the phone. Well, the phone was ringing. The pay phone was ringing at nine o'clock. Nobody would go near the phone and answer it.

We just sat around and obviously we didn't have grief counseling or any of that counseling, but there were a lot of people who came down. Made sure we were all right. I guess that was the first. Obviously that was the death of a fireman or anybody who was a rank, so that was traumatic. To this day I carry that around with me. As a matter of fact, it was really ironic because when the World Trade Center collapsed, obviously everybody's upset, but I was a little screwed up in my head. Didn't know what was going on. I was a little wacky. I just couldn't put ends together about certain things.

About a week and a half after the World Trade Center, George Anderson called me up. I worked with George. I was his captain in One Engine then we went to Six Engine together. He said to me, "Are you all right?" I said, "Yes, I'm fine. What do you mean am I all right?" He says, "Well, the collapse of the World Trade Center, does that bring back anything?" And I says, "You know what George, I've been sitting here for a week and a half, two weeks not knowing what's wrong with me." And it did. Not knowing how it triggered my other thoughts. I said, "You know George, you're really right." We talked for ten minutes about it and then I realized I was in a fog about it and I snapped out of it. But it did bring back, I guess, subconsciously all the bad memories.

There was more to it. He was going to come to my wedding, like I said it was May. The following month, June, I got married, June twenty-fifth.

His wife said he was so much looking forward to my wedding. He never went out with his wife. He couldn't wait to come. I was the first new, young kid he had. He was like a father. He took me under his wing, teaching me.

To this day I believe he saved my life because he took my hook. I say it to everybody and they say "How did he save your life? Did he pull you out of a window?" No, he had my hook and he took my fall. Since that day I've always been a believer, whatever happens, happens for a reason. That's how I was able to cope with it. I honestly believe that now.

Vesey: The night the guys were killed. Russell Schoemer , Vic Lardiere, and Dominick LaTorre got killed. Richie Schoemer got hurt. Freddy Mitchell, he got hurt, down on Astor Street a block below Mulberry, in an old shit out empty building. That was one of our first due boxes.

When we first got there, nothing was going on. Then when they finally realized the guys were in there when the building collapsed, I went into the cellar of one of the joints where some of the guys were. Patty Dougherty was in there helping to get Freddy out. Then Cliff Dainty from Twelve Engine, he got buried. They really uncovered him. The shit dropped on them and they were pinned to the basement floor. They had a lumber yard on them. Police Emergency was there. They didn't have anything to take them out with. They had to lift all that shit up. You couldn't do it manually. They had to put the water and everything else on the God damn thing. The roof fell in. You tried to lift the whole roof up. So, eventually, we got them out. The Police Emergency, they have the hydraulic jacks. Vick Lardiere, he got killed. Dominick LaTorre, nice guy. That was a terrible night, that one there. It was so bad that Chief Grehl even sent us back to quarters.

Everyone was lower than whale shit. We didn't have a drink in the house. Schoemer's father came in. He came up later on. You got to figure, we're all screwed up. What are we going to do? Frank Leber, Captain Leber, he was good. He handled it pretty good. The gin mill across the street, gave us a bottle. Spent the night and the next day, it was like a death in the family, really, as far as feelings and stuff like that. Until they got everything arranged, the funerals and all that. It was three of them. (Very quietly). Schoemer was down the shore. It was tough. Rus was a nice guy. Toughest night, toughest night on the job. Then we all went down, escorted the coffin during funeral, the Honor Guard thing. That was a tough night down there. The bells keep ringing. Guys keep going.

F. Grehl: I can say I'm very, very fortunate in all my time I've never operated at a fire in which we had a death of a firefighter. They always seemed to occur on another tour or something like that which is very, very unfortunate for anyone. Probably the closest I came is when my son went on the fire department and was down in Four Truck. I was a Deputy Chief up in the first division on the same tour and they had that fire on Pennington Street. Russell Schoemer from Five Truck, the captain of Twelve Engine, Dominic LaTorre, and the captain of Four Truck, Vic Lardiere, which was my son's company, were all killed. Captain Lardiere had said to Tommy, "Hey, go outside. Go out and get another hook." He walked out of the building and got another hook. It was so, so, so close. I responded down there out of total concern, obviously. I found out he was all right.

Then Caufield grabbed me and I said, "Is there anything I can do to help?" He said, "Yes, see if you can take charge of the evacuation. We don't know who's been evacuated, who's gone to the hospital, the condition they're in or anything else." So I took that over and went up to the hospital and checked with the captains to find out who was working to see if everyone was accounted for. But that's the closest I came that was on my tour. Other than that I never had any. But naturally, you know all of them. It's hard to accept anybody.

Bobby King, Chief King down in the Second Battalion, he and I went on the fire department together and he was the Battalion Chief at that particular fire where they had the collapse. He had ordered no one to go in that building. It was his order. No one is to go into that building. Of course he has other activities and he walked away. The next thing you know Five Truck and Twelve Engine, what they are, they have to go in and put this thing out for them. Unfortunately, it didn't work out that way. But, Bobby was very shook up over this thing. He had some solace in the thought that, "Hey, I had ordered everybody to stay out of that building and they still went in beyond my orders." But he says, "From now on they will obey my orders or else."

We had a tactical unit at the time. They had a building in which they had had two or three fires and he had ordered nobody in those buildings on his tour. They broadcast it on the radio. They put it in the company journals and everything else. He's making the rounds, so he's not close to the fire that night. He responds down there. He gets to the fire in the building and who's in the building, but the tactical unit. Great guys, tremendous firemen, they have nothing wrong with them. They just got ahead a little bit. But they're in the building. So he gets hold of the captain. He says, "Cap, get hold of your crew. Take up." "What? The thing's a second alarm. What?" He says, "Get your crew and take up." Every fire he had after that, he'd order them up. "Order up the tact unit." Second alarm, "Order up the tact unit." They were never, ever allowed to work at a fire with him again.

Do you know, nobody in City Hall questioned him? The tact unit complained. He said, "They are never allowed to work with me again. I went through that loss of life down there. I ordered nobody to go in that building and I ordered nobody to go in this time. He went beyond my rules. Nobody like that works with me." Sometimes you have to take that extreme a stand in order to wake people up. But they were good men, that tact unit. They were good people.

Charpentier: I thought we could have done more when the collapse was on Pennington and Orchard. We went down on the second alarm. To me it seemed we weren't doing enough and yet it was the proper procedure, what they were doing, when it collapsed and they were lying under all the debris. Everybody wanted to jump in and do. Later on you realize you have to think this thing out first to do it. Then we finally heard muffled sounds, "Get me out of here." We knew that they were still alive. Everybody did dig in, but with a professional organized plan of doing things.

Miller: It was in May of 1972. I was with my wife. We were home watching television. I'll never forget the time. We were watching the eleven o'clock news. My best friend at the time was Captain Dominic LaTorre, who lived on Belair Place. I had worked with him when I first came on the job in 1959. He took me under his wing. He was several years older than I was, but he was a good father and a good firefighter. While watching television that evening, the news flash came out that there were some personnel from the Newark Fire Department trapped on Orchard and Thomas. And I said, "Gee, Dominic's working tonight. Several had been killed. Maybe I should just go down there and check." So, I got dressed and I went down to the fire scene. I got on the scene. They told me that

Captain LaTorre was one of the men who were still trapped in the building. This was about one o'clock in the morning and they were still trying to get him out.

Eventually they got him out and they put him in the ambulance. I went in the ambulance with him. I could see there was no response. He wasn't breathing or anything. He wasn't hurt physically at all that you could see. There were no cuts, no bruises, no scars or anything. What had happened when the roof collapsed his knees went to his chest and evidently he suffocated because he inhaled but he couldn't expel his breathing. So that's probably how he died, from asphyxiation. They tried to give him intravenous, but his veins had already collapsed partially in the ambulance. So we got to the hospital and they did confirm his death.

I, along with several members of the Newark Fire Department, had to go over and tell his wife. We got to his house, we rang the bell, and as soon as she opened the door and she saw that it was I and Chief McCormack she knew there was something wrong. We told her it was Dominic. Of course, the scene after that was unbelievable; the crying and the screaming, the disbelief that that could happen. But when she saw us, she knew that something really bad had happened. At that time his children were young, in grammar school. I think he was forty-two or forty-four at the time. He was on the Battalion Chiefs' list. They gave him a Battalion Chief's funeral because he would have been promoted anyway.

Butler: I was working second tour when you had the three guys die in a fire, Schoemer, LaTorre, and Lardiere. That's tough to hear at all especially when you knew the guys. We worked with Dick Schoemer. Russell was the one who died. We worked with Dick because he was in Five Truck and we ran into them a lot at that time. It was just tough. Why'd they have to die? What the hell did they do wrong? You often wonder, "Geez what can I do so that doesn't happen to me?" You get the straight story from guys who were there plus the official reports and ninety percent of the time I like to talk to guys who were at a scene. Hell, Dick Schoemer was five feet from him. Just happened to be in the right spot where these other three were caught under it all. Dick was badly burned, but he survived. You just hear stories that they were in chasing shit. Guys do that. They don't want to stand around and wait for the fire to burn itself out. We'll put it out so we can go back to the firehouse. We're going to eat dinner or there's something good on TV.

Smith: I remember that building because we used to go in there. We stopped going in there because you could feel the floors just gave when you walked on them. They took out support columns. We never went in there. But I knew all those guys. I went down there. I lived up in Vailsburg. I went down there, but there was nothing they could do. Freddy Mitchell was in Ten Engine on the second tour. I knew the guys, LaTorre, I knew them from One Truck. I used to get a detail down there and I knew them.

Pianka: I was home at the time. The initial reaction is shock, then there's tremendous sadness after a while. I was only there for a couple of years. I knew Russell. Not that well, he was on the second tour. I'm on the third, we're opposite each other. I only see him every eight days if that, so I vaguely know him. After the shock wears off, there's a tremendous sadness. One thing I do remember. I remember going down to the firehouse right after it happened. I remember Hooter being there and he was in shock himself. He was red eyed. You could tell the man was crying. He was a tough guy. He was very upset. We were all upset. We're just like normal people.

It didn't change my view of fighting fires. I don't think it changes most guys'. In the norm there's a sort of fatalism here. We know what we're here for and one of those things is to risk our lives. I think we all understand that at some level. That's what we're getting paid for. There's not much productivity we could show. There's not much we can produce or give. We put fires out and by doing that you're risking your life. I think a lot of guys accept that fact. I'm not going to hold back the next time, because it's a fluke. It ain't going to happen to me.

There had been fires in the building. Somebody took out Lally columns. They converted it into a store on the first floor. That weakened the building. A quirky story I could tell you. Frankie Calvitti was in One Engine at the time. He was on the second tour. He went down there to study with someone. And they were on the roof of an adjoining building to the one that collapsed. He was masking up, just ready to go into the building and the thing fell down before his very eyes. It just goes to show you. A few minutes later, another two three guys could possibly have been killed. One of the fellows was in the basement. Everything missed him. He saw a hole and he scampered out of the basement. The building had collapsed around him. He never got over that. That changed him. But there were quite a few guys there who just said, "That's the way things are." It's your personality I guess.

McGrory: That was a terrible thing where they lost three men. It was in May of '72. The whole building collapsed on them. A number of men were hurt, a few men who really never came back to fire duty. Some who came back but were changed because of it. In June of '72, I took the Fourth

Battalion on the second tour. It was right after the collapse where they lost the three men in the Second Battalion. When I got into the Fourth, some of the men I had were still on injury leave. But most of them had come back. Like Richie Schoemer came back, but he was on light duty for quite a while. He had lost his brother. Plus he had burnt one of his shoulders so badly there was a hole in it. He came back to light duty. He did more as a light duty man in that company than a lot of the regular firefighters did. A few guys from Twelve Engine really got shook up because a number of them were buried there.

So, that was a very, very bad time for them and it was kind of an experience for me coming in there. I had had that building, a fire in that building that collapsed, when I was roving. I was in the Second Battalion. I had that building sometime before then. I remember being in there. I think it was a tavern or something on the first floor that they had cut all up. And it looked like they had taken most of the walls out of the place. That's all I remember of it, but then they must have had multiple fires in that building.

Going in there, I felt a little odd in those houses with those guys. They came back in drips and drabs. I mentioned Schoemer. His brother died. He knew when he died. And he was severely injured, but he came back. How do you deal with it? Everybody has to deal with it in their own way. You talk about family and the fire department being a family. That helps tremendously. You're all together. You'll do anything for your brother firefighter. I think that helps tremendously.

Connell: My first captain was involved in the building collapse where Lardiere, LaTorre, and Schoemer were killed; also Danny Nozza was one of his men. He had a broken leg out of it. Tommy Carroll was another firefighter hurt. He became an operator until he retired after. So my captain was over protective of me. The first working fire I had in a building, he assigned me to assist Charlie Alaimo at the pumps and that's where I stood on the outside, watching everybody else go in. Even during overhaul, I wasn't allowed in. After the fire was completely out, it was time to take up the hose, and then I was allowed to go into the building. The second fire, he conveniently left his mask on the rig. He and John Farrell went in. He told me, go back get his mask and stand by the door until he comes out for it. So the second one I got to stand at the front door and watch everybody run in and out. The third one he finally let me go in. I think I made it to the top of the staircase, feeding the hose as they made their way down the hallway. My job was to make sure there were no kinks in the hose and make sure they had enough hose when they needed it. Finally, about my fifth or sixth fire, I finally entered a fire room with them and about a month or two later I finally got the tip for the first time.

McGee: One of the last fires I went to was the death of Mike DeLane, which was very upsetting to me. We all took Mike's death very hard to say the least. He was a hard worker and a good man.

It was in October. The fire was on Chestnut Street which was notorious for bad fires. I was acting Battalion Chief that night. When the alarm came in, Thirteen Engine with Captain Ricciardi called a working fire and called for a second alarm immediately. By the time I arrived in the chief's car, which is seconds after Thirteen Engine, this house was going. It was a duplex and one half of the duplex was going from top to bottom. The other half was boarded up. Before I even got out of the chief's car, there were neighbors surrounding the car telling me, "There's a woman in there." I remember saying to them, "Well if there's a woman in there my friend.

You better start praying for her." Because there was nobody on the scene and this place was roaring.

Thirteen Engine stretched their line into the building. Nine Engine, which was right behind me, stretch a supply line in and also stretched a line into the building. By that time I had my rubber goods on and I was inside the building with Nine Engine. We were in the first floor of the building where this woman actually died. It was a gas explosion. You could tell because when we got in there I could smell the gas very heavily.

I told the guys from Thirteen Engine to go down the cellar and shut the gas off, which they did. In the mean time, the roof had collapsed on everything in that room, in the dining room. While I was in there we saw this very big bolt. It was just *boom*. I thought a transformer had exploded; this very bluish light. But I was inside the building at the time.

When I came out I could see them bringing Juan Ramos down the ladder. I think Mike was up above him. Then they brought Mike down. All I could do was make sure they got into the ambulance. There were plenty of people around helping. Ramon Irizarry from the Arson Squad actually took a big chance trying to get him down. They got him down and got him to the hospital. Of course the Chief came and relieved me because we had been there for a couple of hours already. I went to the hospital and just stayed at the hospital until the Chaplain came out and told me he had died. That was a very upsetting experience.

But Mike was not the first firefighter who died at a fire where I was working. I was unfortunate enough to be also present when Sal Vacca died. Sal was a new fireman in Eleven Truck. What happened was there was a fire on Eighth Street or Ninth Street, one of those streets right near the firehouse. There was a man trapped on the third floor. Now after the fire is out we found the man's body laying in the door way on the third floor with his arms stretched out. Sal Vacca is laying at the bottom of the stairway with his legs facing up the stairs, which would indicate to me that this man pushed him as he was trying to get out.

In those houses, you went up to the second floor and then you went around to another stairway going to the third floor. Usually there was a door there, too. That door was closed. So what had happened somehow along the line the door got closed after Sal went up those stairs. In any event, Charlie McFadden located Vacca with his mask on, his head down against the door, and his feet pointing up the stairs. At the top of the stairs this man's body was half out of the hallway with his hands stretched out. It would seem to me that Sal made it at least part of the way up there and this guy either knocked him down or something in his rush to get out. That was also a very moving experience.

Marcell: I tell you the saddest thing I ever saw on this job was when Marcus Reddick got killed. That was the saddest thing because that was all unnecessary. We were sitting at the table five minutes before that happened. His mother made me a sweet potato pie because he and I always used to talk. He was doing his college. I think he was studying to be a lawyer. We were going to eat the pie together and a box came in. That's the box he got killed at.

We went down the street. We couldn't get over the street because all the cars, the trucks couldn't get over the street. The cars were parked right to the corner and on half the street the cars were double parked. It was on a Sunday with all those restaurants down there. We had the turn with the gig and we squeezed through. Five Engine came in behind and they could only use a ground ladder. If you could have gotten a truck in there, we could have gotten her out like that. It would have been nothing. We came down the street. They put the ladder up, the ground ladder up on the building. I drove the gig all the way down past the fire building for about ten houses. I came walking back up and the kid sees this woman on a window ledge. He ran up the ladder to make the rescue. The woman was two hundred and twenty five pounds and here was a kid maybe a hundred and sixty pounds honestly.

She faced him and got hold of him. I saw him starting to go over, but I didn't have any boots or anything on. I ran up the ladder to try and help him. When I got there it was too late. She went down. She was sitting on the window sill and somebody opened a door downstairs. They caused a draft and it blew the smoke out over her head and the heat. That's why she fell off. It was just an unfortunate accident that kid got killed. But he tried to do what he was getting paid for, make a rescue. He was a hell of a nice kid. I used to talk with him every day when he went there. He told me some day he wanted to be a lawyer. I don't know if he was ever going to stay on the job or not, but he was a hell of a nice kid.

People say what they would have done if they were there. That's all bullshit. You have to be there. It's the easiest thing in the world for me to criticize what went on, but the kid did what he was getting paid for. He was a good fireman. Could have happened to you or I, but he was just in the wrong spot at the right time. He fell down and next to the front porch there was a concrete support. He fell down where they keep the trash cans and all that kind of stuff. His helmet went off and I had his boot. I grabbed his leg, but you couldn't hold him. The whole ladder went across and hit a window sill. On a brick building the window sills stick out like four inches. Well, the ladder slid over and hit that. As it hit that he went down, the ladder went over. Nobody was footing the ladder. They pulled me back up. I was on the ladder hanging upside down for Christ's sake. I put my leg through it, because I didn't have boots on. If I had boots on, I would have fallen with him, but I only had shoes on. I put my leg through the rung.

Charpentier: When Marcus Reddick died, we were working. I was right there when it happened. It should have never happened. Because there was a language barrier there and this women was nowhere near where flames or smoke were because the fire was in the back of the building and she was in the front. There were people on the ground telling her in Portuguese to jump and we said don't jump because we could have gotten her down. But as Reddick was going up the ladder she jumped, landed on him and they both went down.

There is that feeling that maybe we could have done more when there's a death of a firefighter if we were working; a sense that we didn't do enough. Of course if our tour wasn't working, we really didn't know, but it puts it in the back of your mind that that could have been you.

Smith: The only death that ever bothered me was Hugo Gambacorta. There was a fire on Washington Street. It was a rinky dink fire and it was hot. It had to be a hundred degrees and muggy. We had the Burrells. So, it was two rooms on the second floor. It was smoky. Hugo was in One Truck. He came off the rig. He got in. We got up to the top. We knocked the fire down and after it was knocked down, he was sitting on a burned out bed. So, I was thirsty. I got a drink of water. I says, "What's the matter?" And Hugo said, "I don't feel well?" So I says, "Well, have a drink of water." He says, "No. I feel funny." I says, "Funny funny or bad funny?" He says, "No, I think it's bad funny." I says, "Come on, go downstairs." He stood up. His knees buckled. He went down. I called. The Squad came up and Doctor Ciccone came up. He was dead. I'm trying to think what the hell happened to him? To this day I don't know what killed him, what he died of. But Doctor Ciccone told me that when his knees first bent, he was dead. That's how fast he died. What it was, I don't know.

Dunn: Another event that always stays in my mind; we had a fire on Badger Avenue and Avon several weeks after the Avon Avenue fire. When we rolled out of quarters you could see the sky lit up which was a little bit of a surprise to see the extent of flame in the sky. So, I said, "Geez, here it is again." As we rounded the corner, Ed Dennis, the driver of Eighteen Engine, got out to hook up and had a heart attack and died. That always shocked us because we then fought the fire. Was it the size of the fire or was it the reflection of look what happened on Avon Avenue, it's going to happen again here. Or was it just God's will that he died that night. But he didn't do any work. He stopped the truck, got off, took the soft suction off the truck to hook to the hydrant, and fell down. So, it also made that a memorable fire because it was the only fire I've attended where we had a death of a fireman.

Nobody understood what happened that night because it wasn't what we would consider a fire death. It was a heart attack. But when you reflect back on it, you think about it now. Seeing this type of fire, the amount of fire and the volume of fire, the chances of you getting hurt with a building falling down as you're pulling up, it was a traumatic effect. I realize that today. I didn't realize it at the time. I thought the guy just had a bad heart. But I do realize every fireman who goes to a large fire has some innate reflexes to that fire. What they see and how dangerous what they're doing is. I think that has a telling effect on us not at the incident but later on when we have our stress and heart attacks earlier in life.

Carragher: I went on a fourth alarm when I was in Nine Engine. Joe Buhl was killed at it down on Avenue L and Margaretta at the Engelhorn Meat Packing Plant. He was at Salvage. They had the fire down there early in the morning. They had just gotten to the scene and Joe Buhl told Five Engine to bring a two and a half in the ally. They were going through the ally when the building collapsed on them. The wall came down. He was the only one to get out from under the building from the crew and he was the one who died. I think Alaimo and Tommy Carrol and Danny Nazza were buried under the building.

It took them over an hour to get them out. They were under cinderblocks and steel and everything like that. Unfortunately, Joe Buhl was the one who died. The other three fellows came back on the job. He was crushed. When he crawled out both his arms were broken. Both his legs were broken, but he managed to crawl free from under the debris, just got out of it. He was mangled pretty badly.

Haran: Since I'm on the job, I came on in 1961. Joe Buhl, who was killed four or five months before I came on the job, I took his spot on this job. I'll count Joe Buhl, since I'm on this job there are twenty-four names in my forty years, twenty-four guys were killed in the line of duty. Some guys died at fires, some guys died in the firehouse with heart attacks and they were service connected. There've been twenty-four men. That's twenty-four men too many. If you ever go to a fire department funeral, you never forget it. And I carried a few of them. I carried a few of them as their pallbearers. You'll hear it a million times and you'll see it on the news and television. You'll never forget a fireman's funeral, especially with the bagpipes. They kill you.

But there were some good guys and I carried a few of them to their resting place. Richie Heinze, there were a couple of others. Joe McCarthy I was in on. There were a few of them, good close guys. Some guys I knew just to say hello to. Some guys I didn't know at all. I just knew where they worked and stuff like that. I think, like I said, there were twenty-four guys and not all of them had the chief's funerals. I've been to more than I wanted to be, but I hope guys never have to go to them. The guys you remember like Jimmy Murray, Mike DeLane, Salvatore Vacca, Hugo Gambacorta. Hugo was one of those guys who was in the Academy, who came on eight months after me. He wasn't on too long and he got killed at a fire. He was in One Truck. Sal Vacca, they don't know what happened to him. They found him on a stairway. His tank was expended, but they don't know whether he ran out of air. He was knocked unconscious going up to the second floor. They found him lying on the staircase, Sal Vacca.

Butler: Everybody was devastated the way Mike Moran died. It wasn't in a fire or as the result of a fire. It was just being shot. It was the immediate instant reaction of hate. Hate all the minorities. Hate everybody that's involved in this riot, but as time went on, we had a Director at the time who was quite a religious man. He tried to calm us down, tried to talk to us. One thing led to another and we started to accept, the incident as far as of the guys' attitudes went away. The memory of Mike never did. Guys still think about him from time to time. As a matter of fact even in the new house on Ninth Street the article has a prominent place right by the front door hanging up in a glass enclosed frame, the article of what happened to Mike. But the hate did go away. We always remembered and thought about it. Saying it possibly could happen again, but the initial hate did go away.

I was working the fire when Jimmy Murray died in the Pru building. It was just a set of circumstances. Jimmy's death was tragic because we were able later on to find out we were only about twenty-five feet from him. The way the floor was laid out there were a lot of these portable walls just breaking up cubicles and we were making our way toward what we knew to be the outside wall. We're trying to open some windows up and clear some of the smoke. The smoke was about three quarters of the way down from the ceiling. We finally did find some windows and were able to open them, get some air into the joint. Then we heard a lot of screaming and hollering. The next thing you know there are two guys dragging a guy past us and out into the hallway. They were moving him down to the floor below where the first aid stuff was set up and then to the hospital.

At the time I was the union officer on call. During John Gerow's administration, the way things worked out, one of his officers was always on a tour working between the four tours. And that's the first guy to be called by the operators should somebody need union assistance. Then we'd filter it out and funnel the calls from there to where ever, whether we had to call the president or the vice-president, whoever we had to call. You might just have to call the Chief. A guy's having a problem, I just have to call the Chief and talk to him. But as the union officer on call, I went down; found the Deputy who was Bob Miller. He looked at me, said, "You're the union guy, right? Go ahead." He got his driver to take me up to the hospital.

I was there when they were working him. The hospital personnel all but stood on their head trying to get him back. I mean they were injecting him with shots. They were doing mouth to mouth on him, cardiac massage. Trying everything they could with him, but Jimmy was dead. So, I stayed there and I waited. The family came in. The Director pulled up. The Director looked at me. The family had already gone in the one door. I said,

"He's dead." So, the Director went right in with the family. I tried to be with the family as much as I could. Telling them I'm representing the union until some other guys could get there that were off duty and take over so I could go back to the fire. Just trying to look it over because I was involved then with safety, too. Trying to see.

It was just a tragic chain of events that led to his death. Only from a safety point, the only thing you could see is that he should have left when the other guy left. The other guy on the line had to leave. He should have left, but he chose to stay there. We'll never know why he did that.

Cody: I was at the fire when Jimmy Murray died. I was at that fire. I wasn't in charge of the fire, but I was up on the floor with him and it kind of affected me. Even though I had never even seen him go in and I wasn't working with that company. I was there when we found him. It affected me. I knew Jimmy. He used to be detailed to Six Engine when I was a Captain. He was a nice guy. It's like losing one of the group. Nobody wants that to happen. I think the determination was he had run out of air. That's one of the instances that helped develop the Personal Alarm System. So someone would know you were there if you did run out of air.

It was on the upper floors of the Prudential building where they had all those cubicles all through the building. You were working your way in through them and trying to knock down this fire. The whole floor was involved in fire. I don't know how something like that would have started, but we didn't find him until the smoke cleared.

Prachar: I grew up with Jimmy Murray. His death affected my family. My wife grew up with him, went to school with him. You never know until it hits home how you feel. I pray to God, I mean this sincerely, that I am never in a position where somebody underneath me dies. I don't know if I could handle it. Even now just thinking about it, Jimmy Murray, he died senselessly. Marcus Reddick was attempting a rescue. Schoemer. LaTorre, Lardiere on Orchard Street; how this building had been torn apart, to go in there and die senselessly. I've been to funerals in Boston, Philadelphia. That's like a show of hands. You go there in support of the family. But to have somebody personally, who you know, die in a way he shouldn't have died scares me; scares me to the point that I don't want to see it. Like I said, I don't know how I would handle it mentally, if it was somebody in my command who died. But in the same thought, if the man was doing the job and I was doing my job and it happened maybe so be it. Marcus Reddick died trying to make a rescue, tried to talk to the lady. The lady jumped. He was doing his job. It wasn't a useless death. It was a man performing his duty. Maybe I could handle it mentally, I don't know. It's hard. It's hard.

Jimmy's write up and everything I had plastered on my locker when I was in Rescue. There wasn't a day I went to work that I didn't see that picture and that story, kept that in my mind. I was assigned to his wife the day he was buried, to ride in the limousine with her from the church to the cemetery and back. Memorable? Very much so, very much so, that was probably my worst assignment I ever had to do on this job.

Pianka: When Harry Halpin died, who knew? Who knew the bolts were out? The building came down on the three guys in the early '70s. Who really knew? You walk in and the frigging building came down on you. Even Mike DeLanes's death, kind of weird, you know. How many times people have gone under these wires? Dozens, nothing ever happened, then all of the sudden bingo. But this one with Lawrence Webb, you've got fifteen guys with you. We know what we're doing. This is our bread and butter. How did that happen?

Langenbach: I can remember every one of the firefighter deaths since I've been on the job. I can tell you every one, the circumstances, how they died, where they died, what they were doing when they died. It's a terrible thing. I don't know how guys in New York City are going through it with three hundred and forty-three guys. I remember Harry Halpin when the fire escape collapsed, Harry died. Marcus Reddick, Jimmy Murray, Jimmy Murray was a friend of mine. Another case, shouldn't have happened, should have never died. It shouldn't have come to that. Mike DeLane, the same thing. It goes on and on.

But Larry Webb sticks in my mind because I worked with Willie, his father, and I knew Willie well. Willie and I have maintained that friendship for as long as we've been on the job. To see that happen and to see how simple and nickel dime it was. That should have never happened. To see that nothing was done about it disturbs me. We went tooth and nail with the city over Mike DeLane. That was the first time the union ever sued the city for a wrongful death thing. We went tooth and nail over a couple of other fires, American Refuel, which is a bullshit thing and then Passaic Street another bullshit thing. Yet, we lose a fireman and nobody says anything.

Connell: I was on High Street for two and a half years before I got promoted and maybe six months after. So I was there about three years. I guess that would be around '82, '83 they closed there. Harry Halpin was assigned to the second tour. He was at a Broadway and Third Avenue abandoned building fire on the third floor, and went out on the fire escape. He was pulling the cornice and somebody had removed all the bolts from the fire escape. He fell, fractured his skull and three days later he died in the hospital, which had a very strong effect on me. Eight years earlier we were supposed to swap, he would be alive today. And he was a friend. Everybody on High Street worked together, you were all one big clique. We were the bad boys of the city more or less, but we were the good boys for anybody stationed there. There is a special bond for anybody who has been on High Street.

There was a lot of bitterness. We wrote an article. We all sat down, but Dennis Cogan actually wrote the article that was printed in the paper where we chastised the city for the mayor's and the Fire Director's lack of participation in the funeral or anything to do with Harry. I think that's one of the things that put the nail in the coffin. It was the beginning of the end for High Street after that.

When it's the death of a brother firefighter; that bothers me more than anything else. Anytime anyone of them dies, a piece of you dies. My biggest loss was Harry Halpin. He was a good friend of mine. I came on the job with him. I think his death affected me the most. As a matter of fact, just the past two days I thought about Harry and shed a tear or two for him. Another one that affected me sharply was Jimmy Murray in Twenty-nine Engine. I was working in Seven Truck that night when he died. As a matter of fact I called on the radio about four or five different times, volunteering to go to that fire. There was an out of town company in and they kept on saying, "No, Seven Truck go back to quarters. You're here to be the guide for East Orange."

After they closed High Street down, a little while later, I was demoted for a while, and I went to Fifteen Engine. Then I got promoted back and they changed my tour from fourth tour to the third tour. I roved on the third tour for one full year. Filling firehouse to firehouse and I spent a month in

Twenty-nine Engine working with Jim Murray. I got to know Jim pretty good. I can't say I was close friends with him, but I got to know him fairly good. The idea that he died and it took them a while to find him and nobody knew he was missing. That bothered me for a while.

Marcus Reddick, I never met the man, but there are two things about him that affected me. He was working in my first house, Five Engine, when he died and he was doing a rescue operation. What happened to him could happen to anybody. A woman panicking, she was overweight, she jumped on him. He took the brunt of the force. She survived. He didn't.

The last one that affected me was Joe McCarthy. I was his relief on Twelve Truck for about three, four years. Me and Joe got promoted together off the same list on the same day. We were campaigning for Mayor Gibson, not voluntarily by the way, in the same places the whole day. I met him when I was in Nine Truck. He took me under his wing up there, breaking me in on truck work. During our firefighting careers our paths kept crossing. We were pretty friendly, so when he died that was fairly big loss too.

DeLane, I met the man once or twice. I really didn't know him well, but again he died because he was trying to help another firefighter, especially a new recruit. I believe we are a family and I do look at anybody on the fire department as a member of my family.

Langevin: The death of a firefighter always hurts another firefighter. No matter if he's here in Newark or as far away as San Francisco, any place. It gets you; it really does because you know you do the same thing that he does every day, all day. It hurts, it does. It really hurts. Back in the '70s and '80s, it wasn't uncommon for two hundred firefighters a year to be killed in the line of duty. The one person I knew the closest was a firefighter who came on in my class, Firefighter Harry Halpin. He was the one I knew best. To understand the reason that he died, it made me a little bitter. Harry's death was needless. It was due to vandalism in the building where he stepped on the fire escape. The fire escape had been vandalized for scrap metal. The fire escape pulled away and he fell to his death. To me that's a needless death.

Perdon: Fortunately, I haven't been on the scene when a firefighter has died. If I'm on the scene I don't know, that's a whole new ballgame. I don't know if I could be so stoic or anything. I'll probably be like the biggest baby there. When I go to the funeral, if you see their families there, that's probably when it bothers me more. It's sad. You don't want to see it happen.

List of Interviewees

Baldino, Captain Barney, letter to the author 20 September, 2002. (appointed 1951)

Belzger, Firefighter William, 4 October, 2004, transcript. (appointed 1959)

Bisogna, Captain Joseph, 25 July, 2001, transcript. (appointed 1974)

Butler, Captain James, 3 September, 1993, transcript. (appointed 1963)

Cahill, Firefighter Joseph, 25 June, 1991, transcript. (appointed 1963)

Calvitti, Battalion Chief Frank, 8 July, 2005, transcript. (appointed 1966)

Carragher, Deputy Chief William, November 1994, transcript. (appointed 1960)

Carter, Battalion Chief Harry, 12 June, 1991, transcript. (appointed 1973)

Charpentier, Firefighter Frederick, 22 August 1993, transcript. (appointed 1959)

Cody, Battalion Chief James, 26 October 1999, transcript. (appointed 1964)

Connell, Battalion Chief Anthony, 26 February, 1999, 24 November, 2003. (appointed 1974)

Cosby, Firefighter Joseph, 22 August, 1991, transcript. (appointed 1969)

Denvir, Captain John, 13 September 1993, transcript. (appointed 1959)

Deutch, Firefighter Charles, 14 November 1993, transcript. (appointed 1953)

Doherty, Captain Patrick, 18 20, September, 2000, transcript. (appointed 1970)

Dunn, Deputy Chief Edward, 14 August1991, 29 August 1997, transcript. (appointed 1959)

Finucan, Deputy Chief James, 7 August 1991, transcript. (appointed 1969)

Freda, Deputy Chief Alfred, 12, 25, 26 July 1991, transcript. (appointed 1959)

Fredette, Firefighter Reggie, 3 November, 1993, transcript. (appointed 1942)

Freeman, Captain Richard, 20, 21 August 1991, transcript. (appointed 1956)

Garrity, Battalion Chief Joseph, May 1992, transcript. (appointed 1964)

Gesualdo, Captain Al, 21 July, 2003, transcript. (appointed 1978)

Grehl, Deputy Chief Frederick, 7 August 1993, transcript. (appointed 1948)

Grehl, Captain Thomas, 29 May, 2002, transcript. (appointed 1971)

Griffith, Chief Fire Alarm Operator Robert, 3 July, 1991, transcript. (appointed 1953)

Haran, Captain Edward, 5 February 2001, transcript. (appointed 1961)

Harris, Captain William, 13 December 1999, transcript. (appointed 1961)

Highsmith, Firefighter Gerald, 2 June 1994, transcript. (appointed 1963)

Kinnear, Deputy Chief David, 28 September 1992, transcript. (appointed 1947)

Knight, Firefighter Gerald, 19 June 1991, transcript. (appointed 1964)

Langenbach, Deputy Chief James, 24 October, 2002, transcript. (appointed 1973)

Langevin, Firefighter Robert, 23 February, 1999, transcript. (appointed 1974)

Luxton, Captain Charles, 14 January, 1999, transcript. (appointed 1973)

Marcell, Firefighter Andrew, 23 September 1998, transcript. (appointed 1959)

Masters, Firefighter Anthony, 24 March, 2004, transcript. (appointed 1947)

Masterson, Captain Andrew, 6 April, 2005, transcript. (appointed 1949)

McCormack, Sr. Deputy Chief James, 14 June 1991, transcript. (appointed 1949)

McDonnell, Captain Thomas, 30 March, 1999, 16 April, 1999, transcript. (appointed 1970)

McGee, Captain Raymond, 26 October 2000, transcript. (appointed 1956)

McGovern, Battalion Chief Thomas, 8 June, 2001, transcript. (appointed 1968)

McGrory. Deputy Chief Albert, 31 August 1991, transcript. (appointed 1957)

Miller, Battalion Chief Joseph, 16, 21 August 1991, transcript. (appointed 1959)

Perdon, Captain George, 9 June, 2003, transcript. (appointed 1974)

1970) Pianka, Firefighter George, 15 June, 2001, transcript. (appointed 1970)

Pignato, Captain Nicholas, 26 May, 1999, transcript. (appointed 1974)

Prachar, Captain Daniel, 12 August, 1991, transcript. (appointed 1968)

Redden, Fire Chief Joseph, 16 September 2002, transcript. (appointed 1947)

Ricca, Battalion Chief Ronald, 1 June, 2000, transcript. (appointed 1974)

Rotonda, Firefighter Gerard, 3 May, 2000, transcript. (appointed 1970)

Ryan, Battalion Chief Joseph, 28 September, 1999, transcript. (appointed 1973)

Schoemer, Firefighter Richard, 1 July, 2005, transcript. (appointed 1959)

Smith, Firefighter James, 2 September 1998, transcript. (appointed 1959)

Stoffers, Battalion Chief Carl, 2 September 1998, transcript. (appointed 1956)

Vesey, Firefighter Edward, 15 June 1999, transcript. (appointed 1948)

Vetrini, Captain Joseph, 14 September, 1993, transcript. (appointed 1946)

Wall, Deputy Chief Edward, 13 September, 2000, transcript. (appointed 1954)

Wargo, Captain Andrew, 6 June 1991, transcript. (appointed 1964)

www.ingramcontent.com/pod-product-compliance
Lightning Source LLC
Chambersburg PA
CBHW030011110426
42741CB00032B/272